THE CATHOLIC UNIVERSITY OF AMERICA
CANON LAW STUDIES

THE BISHOP'S QUINQUENNIAL REPORT

A HISTORICAL SYNOPSIS AND A COMMENTARY

A DISSERTATION

Submitted to the Faculty of the School of Canon Law of the Catholic University of America in Partial Fulfillment of the Requirements for the Degree of Doctor of Canon Law

by the

REVEREND JAMES J. CARROLL, A.B., J.C.L.
Priest of the Diocese of Columbus

THE CATHOLIC UNIVERSITY OF AMERICA PRESS
WASHINGTON, D. C.
1956

NIHIL OBSTAT:
CLEMENT BASTNAGEL, J.U.D.
Censor Deputatus

Washingtonii, D.C., die 23 maii 1955

IMPRIMATUR:
✠ MICHAEL J. READY, D.D.
Episcopus Columbensis

Columbi, die 18 maii 1955

Printed by The Abbey Press, St. Meinrad, Indiana, U.S.A.

RESPECTFULLY DEDICATED
WITH
REVERENCE AND GRATITUDE
TO
HIS EXCELLENCY
THE MOST REVEREND MICHAEL J. READY, D.D.
BISHOP OF COLUMBUS

TABLE OF CONTENTS

Part Two

CANONICAL COMMENTARY

CHAPTER III

CHAPTER IV

CHAPTER V

CHAPTER VI

FOREWORD

Among the chief duties which the Code of Canon Law imposes upon every residential bishop is the obligation of submitting a quinquennial report to the Holy See on the spiritual and material condition of his diocese. This dutiful action exists as a bond of reverence and obedience to the Apostolic See. It originates from the rights which the Supreme Pontiff possesses in virtue of the primacy he enjoys over the universal Church.

The Sovereign Pontiff, like Peter, has been commissioned by Christ with the words: "Feed My lambs; feed My sheep." In order that he may properly fulfill that command, he must know well the flock committed to his care. It is of absolute necessity, therefore, that there be established for him the possibility of a free and expeditious contact with the universal Church. To attain that goal, determined by God Himself, the Holy Father must enjoy the right of demanding that all bishops inform him about the status of the subjects under their jurisdiction.

The purpose of the quinquennial report is manifest. Its principal intent is to effect a closer union between the universal Church and the Papacy. The necessity of presenting a regular report brings bishops into a more intimate relationship with their supreme head, prompts them to keep a closer watch over the spiritual welfare of their subjects, and at the same time actuates them to a keener sense of duty.

This obligation, the fulfillment of which the canons demand and the bishops themselves promise under oath, is of the utmost importance. As many Popes have demonstrated, it is upon this obedience of the bishops to the Apostolic See that the entire unity of the Church rests, that the communion of saints will be strengthened, and that the threat of heresies and schisms can be lessened.

The performance of that duty is in a true sense a link with the past. A blessed companionship arises between the bishops of the present and their brother priests of preceding centuries. They join Paul, Irenaeus, Ambrose, Augustine, Francis de Sales, John Carroll and Giuseppe Sarto in pronouncing their obedience and reverence to Christ's Vicar on earth.

The purpose of this dissertation is first to explore the historical development of so important an episcopal duty, and then to present a canonical commentary on the law now contained in canon 340.

Canonical tradition has always treated the quinquennial report and the *ad limina* visit as a single subject, so that legislation regarding the one has inevitably affected that of the other. For that reason, a treatment of the quinquennial report, particularly in the historical conspectus, has necessitated a simultaneous study of the background of the law obliging bishops to visit the Eternal City at stated intevals.

The writer welcomes this occasion to acknowledge his sincere gratitude to His Excellency, the Most Reverend Michael J. Ready, D.D., Bishop of Columbus, for the opportunity of graduate study in Canon Law at the Catholic University of America. An expression of deep appreciation is extended also to the Faculty of the School of Canon Law for their helpful suggestions and scholarly guidance, and to all others whose kindness and encouragement have made this dissertation possible.

DEFINITION AND ETYMOLOGY OF TERMS

ARTICLE I. THE *Ad Limina* VISIT

The *ad limina* visitation is a generic expression which designates a threefold act, each part distinct from the other and yet intimately connected with it by reason of purpose and time of fulfillment.[1]

The majority of canonists have interpreted these acts or obligations in this manner: 1 a) the visit to the basilica of Saint Peter, situated in the Vatican, and to that of Saint Paul, situated on the Via Ostiense, for the purpose of praying at the tombs of the princes of the Apostles; 1 b) the inscribing of their names on a register kept in the sacristies of the two basilicas, and receiving documents to be presented to the Consistorial Congregation as proof of their visit; 2) a personal visit to the Sovereign Pontiff, which includes the acts of homage and obedience to Christ's Vicar on earth, and the presenting of an oral report regarding the status of their diocese, along with words of counsel from the Pope, and on their own part the offering of any suggestions in reference to ecclesiastical discipline if such are requested; 3) a submitting of the written report relative to the administration of their jurisdiction to the Consistorial Congregation, and in the case of missionary countries to the Congregation for the Propagation of the Faith.[2]

[1] Beste, *Introductio in Codicem* (3. ed., Collegeville, Minn.: St. John's Abbey Press, 1946), p. 273 (hereafter cited as Beste).

[2] Wernz-Vidal, *Ius Canonicum ad Normam Exactam* (7 vols. in 8, Vol. II, 3. ed., A. P. Philippo Aguirre, S.I., recognita, Romae: Apud Aedes Universitatis Gregorianae, 1943), Vol. II *De Personis*, n. 605 (hereafter cited as Wernz-Vidal); Ferreres, *Institutiones Canonicae* (2. ed., 2 vols., Barcinonae; Eugenius Subipina, 1920), I, n. 657 (hereafter cited as Ferreres); Coronata, *Institutiones Iuris Canonici* (5 vols., Vol. I, 2. ed., Taurini-Romae: Marietti, 1939), I, n. 399 (hereafter cited as Coronata); Bouix, *Tractatus de Episcopo* (2 vols.,

The expression *limina Apostolorum,* whenever used in an ecclesiastical sense from the earliest days of the Church to the time of the Code, has always been understood to indicate the basilicas or tombs of the Apostles Peter and Paul.

Etymologically, the singular form, *limen,* signifies threshold or door. Virgil (70-19 B.C.) used it in the sense of entrance. Approved lexicons also defines this word with a secondary meaning of *house, dwelling,* or *abode,* and it was in this sense that Livy (59 B.C.-17 A.D.) made mention of it.[3]

From this general definition of *house* or *dwelling,* the word *limen* came to be understood in ecclesiastical terminology as a church building or basilica, and had particular reference to the basilicas where the remains of Saints Peter and Paul were entombed in Rome.[4]

The canonical expression, *visitare limina Apostolorum,* therefore, came to be used as designating the obligation imposed on residential bishops to visit the basilicas or tombs of the Apostles Peter and Paul.[5]

Article II. The Quinquennial Report

The official report of the administration of their diocese,

Parisiis: Apud Jacobum Lecoffre et Socios, Bibliopolas, 1859), II, 45 (hereafter cited as Bouix; Augustine, *A Commentary on the New Code of Canon Law* (8 vols., Vol. II, 3. ed., St. Louis: Herder, 1919), II, 367 (hereafter cited as Augustine); Cappello, *De Visitatione SS. Liminum et Dioeceseon* (2 vols., Vol. I, Romae, Pustet, 1912), I, 1 (hereafter cited as *De Visitatione*).

[3] Andrews, *A Copious and Critical Latin-English Lexicon* (Founded on the "*Larger Latin German Lexicon*" of Wm. Freund, New York: Harper & Bros., 1870), p. 886; A. Forcellini, J. Facciolati et J. Furlanetti, *Lexicon Totius Latinitatis* (5 vols., Patavii, 1871), Vol. I, *Limen*, p. 88.

[4] Du Cange, *Glossarum Mediae et Infimae Latinitatis,* conditum a Corolo du Fresne Domino du Cange, Auctum a Monachis Ordinis S. Benedicti, editio nova a *Leopold* Favre (6 vols., Parisiis, 1933). Reprint, (Vols. I-II, 1937, Vols. III-X, 1938), Vol. V, *Limen,* p. 112.

[5] André-Wagner, *Dictionnaire de Droit Canonique* (5. ed., 3 vols. and supplement, Paris, 1901), Vol. II, *Limina Apostolorum,* p. 541.

which all ordinaries are obliged to submit to the Sovereign Pontiff, is commonly known as the Quinquennial Report. It obtains its name from the law of the Code which prescribes that it is to be submitted every five years.[6]

It has not always been obligatory to present this report every *five* years, and accordingly papal constitutions have usually referred to it as the *Relatio Status Ecclesiarum.*[7]

The Code speaks of this duty as the *"relatio de suo . . . pastorali officio . . ."* and the *"relatio . . . super statu dioecesis."*[8]

It is of obligation for all ordinaries to draw up this report every five years and submit it to the Holy See. In it they outline the status of their diocese, and they prepare it according to the formula prescribed by the Apostolic See.[9] This *relatio* follows a formula established by a decree of the Sacred Consistorial Congregation, November 4, 1918.[10]

[6] Canon 340, § 1.

[7] Cf. Sixtus V, const. *Romanus Pontifex,* 20 dec. 1585—*Codicis Iuris Canonici Fontes,* cura Emi Card. Petri Gasparri editi (9 vols., Romae postea Civitate Vaticana: Typis Polyglottis Vaticanis, 1923-1939; Vols, VII, VIII, IX, cura et studio Emi Card. Iustiniani Serédi), n. 156 (hereafter cited as *Fontes*); Benedictus XIV, const. *Quod Sancta,* 23 nov. 1740—*Fontes,* n. 303; S.C.C., decr. *A remotissima,* 31 dec. 1909—*Fontes,* n. 2064.

[8] Canon 340, § 1.

[9] *Loc. cit.*

[10] *Acta Apostolicae Sedis, Commentarium Officiale* (Romae, 1909-1929; Civitate Vaticana, 1929—) X (1918), 487-503 (hereafter cited as *AAS*); Bouscaren, *The Canon Law Digest* (3 vols., Milwaukee, Wisconsin: The Bruce Publishing Co., 1934-1943-1954), I, 202 (hereafter cited as *Digest*).

PART ONE

HISTORY OF THE QUINQUENNIAL REPORT

CHAPTER I

HISTORICAL DEVELOPMENT PRIOR TO THE SIXTEENTH CENTURY

ARTICLE I. THE VISIT AND REPORT PRIOR TO THE COUNCIL OF ROME (743)

Section 1. Custom

No particular year nor any act of legislation can be set down as marking the starting point of the obligation of making the *ad limina* visit and of submitting the quinquennial report. It was a process of gradual development, but nonetheless a practice known and followed throughout the centuries, finding its basic truth in Christ's deputation of Peter and of every one of his lawful successors as His Vicar on earth. Historical evidences demonstrate, however, that even when the Church was in its infancy it was an accepted custom for bishops to visit the Sovereign Pontiff and to report to him on important matters relative to the administration of their churches. From the beginning, bishops recognized the need and utility of conferring with the Holy Father—of apprising Christ's Vicar on earth of such serious problems as affected the Church and of seeking his advice and direction.[1]

The primacy of the Bishop of Rome was a generally accepted doctrine in the universal Church, and hence it was only natural that when difficulties arose, and when ecclesiastical matters that needed true and infallible decisions presented themselves, the only logical course to follow was

[1] Lucidi, *De Visitatione Sacrorum Liminum* (3. ed., a Josepho Schneider, 3 vols., Romae, 1883), I, 18 (hereafter cited as Lucidi).

to submit them to the visible head of the Church. Just as the Apostles turned to Christ for direction and help, so too their successors, the bishops, had recourse to the Pope, Christ's official representative.[2]

Probably the first recorded instance of a visit made to a supreme Pontiff for such a purpose is that of St. Paul. Shortly after his miraculous conversion, the Apostle of the Gentiles visited St. Peter, not to learn the Gospel but to demonstrate his respect for the leader of Christ's Church.[3]

Historical records demonstrate that the Popes exercised their right of primacy over the universal Church[4] and that the prelates acknowledged this prerogative by visiting the Pope and submitting reports when they were requested to do so.[5]

During this early period, however, there was no general obligation which imposed upon bishops the duty of performing the visitation or of giving a report at determined intervals.[6]

Section 2. Conciliar Legislation

The first vestiges of the obligation of making the visitation and of submitting a report are found in the very ancient practice of holding *provincial councils* twice a year. That practice was an outgrowth of the legislation of the I General Council of Nicaea, held in 325. A matter of

[2] Thomassinus, *Vetus et Nova Ecclesiae Disciplina* (3 vols., Magontiaci, 1787, Pars II, lib. III, cap. XL nn. 8, 9 (hereafter cited as Thomassinus); Benedictus XIV, *De Synodo Dioecesana* (2. ed., 2 vols., Parmae, 1764), Lib. XIII, cap. 6, n. 1.

[3] Epistle of St. Paul to the Galatians: I, 18.

[4] Denzinger-Bannwart-Umberg, *Enchiridion Symbolorum, Definitionum et Declarationum de Rebus Fidei et Morum* (10. ed., Friburgi Brisgoviae: Herder, 1908), n. 41; Eusebius, *Historia Ecclesiastica*, Lib. V, cap. 6—J. P. Migne, *Patrologiae Cursus Completus, Series Graeca* (161 vols., Parisiis, 1857-1866), XX, 446 (hereafter cited as *MPG*).

[5] Eusebius, *Historia Ecclesiastica*, Lib. V, cap. 3—*MPG*, XX, 438.

[6] Cappello, *De Visitatione*, I, 5.

particular importance to the Fathers of the Council was the regulating of church discipline. They especially had in mind the establishing of definite norms with reference to such elements as related to the inflicting or the incurring of excommunications, so that justice and equity might be uniformly applied throughout the Church. To accomplish this purpose, the Council decided that for a proper investigation of whether a censure was rightfully imposed by a bishop, it seemed proper to decree that in each province two synods be held annually, so that through a general assembly of all the bishops of a province such an investigation might be undertaken.[7]

In retrospect, that legislation may in truth be termed the beginning of the law from which the *ad limina* visit and the quinquennial report were to develop as obligations for the hierarchy.

It should be remembered, however, that this canon of the Council of Nicaea was concerned primarily with the "business of investigating cases of alleged unjust excommunication."[8]

A decree of the I Council of Constantinople (381), however, gave a further interpretation to the mind of the Fathers of the Nicene Council when it was decided that ". . . if the rule prescribed for the decrees be observed, it is clear that in every eparchy (province) the affairs are to be managed by the eparchal synod, according to the Nicene decisions."[9]

The legislation of the IV Ecumenical Council, held at Chalcedon in 451 during the pontificate of Pope Leo the

[7] I General Council of Nicaea (325), c. 5—Hardouin, *Acta Conciliorum et Epistolae Decretales ac Constitutiones Summorum Pontificum* (12 vols., Parisiis, 1714-1715), I, 323 (hereafter cited as Hardouin); Bruns, *Canones Apostolorum et Conciliorum Saeculorum IV-VII* (2 vols., Berolini, 1839), I, 15 (hereafter cited as Bruns).

[8] Schroeder, *Disciplinary Decrees of the General Councils* (St. Louis: B. Herder Book Co., 1937), p. 29.

[9] I General Council of Constantinople (381), canon 2—Hardouin, I, 819.

Great, was even more clear and explicit about the holding of *provincial councils.*[10]

In accordance with these decrees, the Pope as Metropolitan and as Primate of all Italy convoked councils for the province of Rome. All the suffragan bishops of the Roman Province, inclusive of Sicily and Sardinia, were obliged to attend these sessions held in the Eternal City.[11]

Metropolitans of areas outside the province of Rome convoked similar councils for their suffragan bishops.[12]

But the Metropolitan of Rome possessed a unique position among the other metropolitans of the Church. Not only were meetings to be held in each provincial district but a report of the deliberations was to be sent to the Supreme Metropolitan—the Pope of Rome. This is clear from a resolution adopted by the Council of Sardica in the year 343: "Hoc enim optimum et valde congruentissimum esse (videtur), si ad caput, id est, ad Petri Apostolicam Sedem, de singulis quibusque provinciis domini *referant* sacerdotes.[13]

Further proof that such a practice was followed at this early time is evident from a declaration which the Fathers of the General Council of Ephesus (431) made and in which they expressed their decision on the necessity of provincial councils to Pope Celestine I (422-432).

The real significance of the letter is understood when it is noted that the decision emanated from a General Coun-

[10] General Council of Chalcedon (451), canon 19: "Statuit igitur haec sancta synodus secundum patrum regulas bis in anno in unum convenire, per singulas provincias, episcopos."—Hardouin, II, 610.

[11] Thomassinus, Pars II, lib. III, cap. XL, nn. 8, 9; Catalanus, *Pontificale Romanum* (3 vols., Parisiis, 1850), Pars I, cap. IX, n. 9 (hereafter cited as Catalanus).

[12] Council of Antioch (343), canon 20—Hardouin, I, 601; Council of Carthage (401), canon 10—Hardouin, I, 998; II Council of Arles (452), canon 19—Hardouin, II, 773.

[13] Hardouin, I, 653. More than fourteen hundred years later, Pope Benedict XIV incorporated that very statement in his Constitution *Quod Sancta,* which proclaimed the obligation of making the *ad limina* visit and of submitting a report.—*Fontes,* n. 303.

[14] Hardouin, I, 1503.

cil of the Church, held in an early century. It indicated, therefore, that even at that time the making of a visit and the submitting of a report to the Pope—though not a law, as such—was truly encouraged among the bishops.

Section 3. Influence of Pope Leo I

Some of the more important evidence relative to the history of the *ad limina* visit and the quinquennial report is found in the letters of Pope Leo I (440-461).

An indication of the antiquity of the practice can be found in a letter written in 440 in which the Pope addressed a message to the bishops of the Province of Vienne. In it he lauded them for their faithful adherence to what he termed the *ancient custom of submitting reports to the Holy See.*[15]

Again, in 447, the same Pontiff in writing to all the bishops of Sicily reminded them of their duty of attendance at the Roman Provincial Councils. The Pope declared that the Councils (Nicaea, etc.), had ordered biannual meetings for every province. As the Metropolitan of the Roman province, the Pope recognized the length of time involved in journeying to Rome twice a year. With that in mind and to obviate the possibility of the emergence of any errors or scandals as a result of the bishops' absence, Pope Leo I relaxed the regulation. Thereafter, he decreed, the bishops of Sicily were permitted to send three of their number to the council which was to be held *each year* during the autumn in the Eternal City.[16]

Section 4. Influence of Pope Gregory I

A further relaxation of the duty of attendance at the

[15] *Epistolae Papae Leonis I,* ep. 10—Migne, *Patrologiae Cursus Completus, Series Latina* (221 vols., Parisiis, 1844-1864), LIV, 634 (hereafter cited as *MPL*).

[16] *Epistolae Papae Leonis I,* ep. 6—*MPL,* LIV, 702, 724; Jaffé, *Regesta Pontificum Romanorum ab condita ecclesia ad annum post Christum natum MCXCVIII* (2. ed., G. Wattenbach, F. Kaltenbrunner, P. Ewald, S. Loewenfeld, 2 vols., Lipsiae, 1885-1888), JK, 414 (hereafter cited as JK, JE, JL).

Roman Provincial Councils occurred sometime between the years 447-590. Just when and in consequence of which events this was brought about, historians have been unable to determine. This much is true, however, that in 590 Pope Gregory I (590-604), when writing to his legate, Cyprian the Deacon, declared that attendance at the Roman Provincial Councils was to be obligatory only *once every five years* for the bishops of Sicily, instead of *once every three years,* as had been the discipline.[17]

Gregory wished also to make other provisions for these suffragan bishops in order to reduce the time of absence from their dioceses. To accomplish that, he appointed Maximian, Bishop of Syracuse, as his vicar or legate in Sicily. As the official representative of the Metropolitan of Rome (the Pope), Maximian could advert to and settle many of the problems of the bishops of that area. Affairs of major import, however, were still to be sent to the Sovereign Pontiff.[18]

It is the opinion of authors generally, that it was from this practice of holding provincial councils for the suffragan bishops of the Roman Pronvice—as initiated in the Nicene legislation—that the law regarding the making of the *ad limina* visit and the submitting of a quinquennial report had its origin.[19]

[17] *Epistolae Papae Gregorii I,* lib. 7, ep. 22—*MPL,* LXXVII, 875.

[18] *MPL,* LXXVII, 543.

[19] Thomassinus, Pars II, lib. III, cap. XLII, n. 1; Vermeersch-Creusen, *Epitome Iuris Canonici* (3 vols., Vol. I, 7. ed., 1949; Vol. II, 6. ed., 1940; Vol. III, 6. ed., 1946, Mechliniae-Romae: H. Dessain), I, n. 457 (hereafter cited as *Epitome*); Wernz-Vidal, II, n. 608; Cappello did not indicate the source of his information, but he stated that, while the bishops were in Rome to attend these councils, it was customary to venerate the tombs of the Apostles Peter and Paul. Moreover, during the conciliar sessions, it became an accepted procedure for the prelates to give a report concerning their respective dioceses.—*Summa Iuris Canonici* (3 vols., Vols. I & II, 4. ed., 1945; Vol. III, 1940, Romae: Apud Aedes Universitatis Gregorianae), I, n. 383 (hereafter cited as *Summa Iuris*).

ARTICLE II. LEGISLATION OF THE COUNCIL OF ROME (743)

Section 1. Law Obliging Bishops to Attend the Roman Provincial Councils

One of the more important acts of legislation affecting the obligation implied in the *ad limina* visit and in the submitting of a report emanated from the Council of Rome, convened in 743 under the direction of Pope Zachary (741-752).[20]

The Fathers of this Council bound a new group of bishops to the obligation of attendance at the Roman councils, namely those who had received their episcopal consecration from the Holy Father. Such members of the hierarchy were to come to the Council held in Rome every year around the Ides of May, if their dioceses were near the province of Rome. If their dioceses were more remote, the hierarchs were to pay their visit to the Eternal City according to the time specified in the certificate which they signed at the time of their consecration.[21]

[20] Council of Rome (743), c. 4: "Ut iuxta sanctorum patrum et canonum statuta, omnes episcopi qui huius Apostolicae Sedis ordinationi subiacebunt, qui propinqui sunt, omnes Idibus Maii sanctorum principum Apostolorum Petri et Pauli liminibus praesententur, omni occasione seposita. Qui vero de longinquo, iuxta chirographum suum impleant. Nam qui huius constitutionis contemptor exstiterit, praeter si aegritudine valida fuerit detentus, sciat se canonibus subiacere."—*Monumenta Germaniae Historica*, Legum Sectio III, *Concilia*, Tomus II, *Concilia Aevi Karolini.* (recensuit A. Werminghoff, Hannoverae et Lipsiae: Impensis Bibliopolii Hahniani, 1896), p. 13 (hereafter cited as *MGH, Conc.*); Hardouin, III, 1827; Mansi, *Sacrorum Conciliorum Nova et Amplissima Collectio* (53 vols. in 60, Parisiis, 1901-1927), XII, 382 (hereafter cited as Mansi).

[21] "Episcopi vero, qui ordinationi apostolicae subiacent, etiam hanc reverentiam debent, ut singulis annis apostolorum liminibus sese repraesentent."—Paucapalea, *Summa des Paucapalea über das Decretum Gratiani* (ed. by J. F. von Schulte, Giessen: Roth, 1890), p. 47; "Illi vero episcopi, qui sunt in provincia Romanae ecclesiae vel ab eo consecrationem accipiunt, eam reverentiam debent papae, ut singulis annis ipsum visitent; si autem aliqui de longinquo sunt, ei se per literas commendent."—Rufinus, *Die Summa Decretorum des Magister Rufinus* (edidit H. Singer, Paderborn: Ferdinand Schoningh, 1902), p. 194 (hereafter cited as *Summa Decretorum*).

This was not a universal law for each and every bishop of the entire Church; still it was wider in scope than any previous legislation. Prior to this enactment, the duty of attendance at the provincial councils of Rome was obligatory only for the bishops of the province. As a result of this legislation, however, not only were the suffragans of the Metropolitan of Rome bound to come to Rome periodically, but also all bishops who had been consecrated by the Pope, were obliged to be present unless lawfully excused. Furthermore, if other metropolitans had been consecrated by the Pope or had received the pallium from him, they were also bound.[22]

At this period of history, the Holy See had not as yet reserved to itself exclusively the right of consecrating bishops. Therefore, as Thomassinus (1619-1695) concluded, bishops who were consecrated by their own metropolitans were not obligated by this new law. It was out of their own devotion, or for the fulfillment of a private vow, or in answer to a personal summons from the Sovereign Pontiff, that bishops felt impelled to make a visit to Rome.[23]

The authorship of this canon, which so widely affected this particular disciplinary practice among the bishops, was a matter of much dispute among commentators. In the common editions of the *Decretum Gratiani,* this canon was ascribed to Pope Anacletus (76-88) as well as to Pope Zachary (741-752).[24]

The entire argument, based on the assumption that the decretals incorporated in the Pseudo-Isidorian Collection were genuine, may be abandoned today. Fagnanus (1588-1678) and Ferraris (1688-1763) were among the chief proponents who looked to Pope Anacletus for the authorship of this regulation.[25]

[22] Thomassinus, Pars II, lib. III, cap. XL, n. 10.

[23] *Ibid.,* cap. XLI, n. 12.

[24] C. 4, D. XCIII.

[25] Fagnanus, *Ius Canonicum seu Commentaria Absolutissima in Quinque Libros Decretalium* (5 vols., in 3, Venetiis: apud Paulum

It was the opinion of most commentators, however, that this canon originated as positive legislation in the Decrees of the Council of Rome, convoked in 743 under the direction of Pope Zachary (741-752). These canonists interpreted the words "*sanctorum patrum et canonum statuta*" of canon 4, Distinction XCIII, as referring to canon 5 of the I General Council of Nicaea (325); to canon 2 of the I General Council of Constantinople (381, and to canon 19 of the General Council of Chalcedon (451).[26]

Moreover, that conclusion is given added authority when it is noted that the disputed canon is always placed with the Decrees of the Council of Rome by well known compilers of various pontifical and conciliar legislation.[27]

Section 2. Interpretation of the Law

> Ut iuxta sanctorum patrum et canonum statuta, omnes episcopi qui huius Apostolicae Sedis ordinationi subiacebunt, qui propinqui sunt, omnes Idibus Maii sanctorum principum Apostolorum Petri et Pauli liminibus praesententur, omni occasione seposita. Qui vero de longinquo, iuxta chirographum suum impleant. Nam qui huius constitutionis contemptor exstiterit, praeter si aegritudine valida fuerit detentus, sciat, se canonibus subiacere.

With reference to the juridical interpretation which canonists of the twelfth and thirteenth centuries attached to

Ballennium, 1709), tit. XXIV, *de iureiurando*, n. 3 (hereafter cited as Fagnanus); Ferraris, *Prompta Bibliotheca Canonica, Iuridica, Moralis, Theologica, nec non Ascetica, Polemica, Rubristica, Historica* (ed. novissima, 9 vols., Romae, 1885-1899), Vol. V, s.v. *Limen Apostolorum*, n. 2 (hereafter cited as Ferraris).

[26] Berardi, *Gratiani Canones* (3 vols. in 4, Venetiis: Ex Typographia Petri Valvensis, 1778), II, cap. 69, p. 171; Benedictus XIV, *De Synodo Dioecesana*, Lib. XIII, cap. 6, n. 12; Thomassinus, Pars II, lib. III, cap. XLI, n. 12; Wernz-Vidal, II, n. 606; Bouix, I, 47; Lucidi, I, 9.

[27] *MGH, Conc.*, Tom. II, *Concilia Aevi Karolini*, p. 13: Hardouin, III, 1927; Mansi, XII, 382; *Anselmi Lucensis Collectio Canonum, una cum Collectione Minore iussu Instituti Savignani* (2 vols., recensuit F. Thaner, Oeniponte: Libraria Academiae Wagnerianae, 1906-1915), Vol. II, lib. VII, c. 150, p. 338.

canon 4, Distinction XCIII, it is important to note that in the immediately preceding canon[28] Gratian cited the general norm that all bishops who were immediately subject to the Pope were to demonstrate their filial affection for him by way of yearly visits to the Pontifical Curia. This stood as a prelude to the obligation canonically established in canon 4. Therein it was decreed that those bishops who received their consecration from the Roman Pontiff and by reason of that were immediately subject to him, were to visit the tombs of the Apostles either in person or through a delegate every year. This obligation rested with these bishops if their diocese was near, i.e., to the provincial limits of Rome. If their diocese was quite distant from the provincial limits of Rome, they were to follow the procedure established in the certificate which they signed at the time of their consecration.

The Glossator defined "intra" as being 'near to' those prelates who lived within the province of Rome.[30] In other words the legislation was repeating the old law which had always obligated suffragans of the Roman province to attendance at the meetings. The new element of the law, however, bound that group of bishops who, although they lived outside the province of Rome, attended the Roman provincial councils because they had been consecrated by the Pope—the Metropolitan of Rome! To substantiate that explanation, Ioannes Teutonicus (†1245) made reference to a decision handed down by Emperor Justinian (527-565) in the problem of prescription.[31]

The canon permitted bishops to make the visit either personally or by way of an authorized delegate. The latter prerogative was based on the assumption that the prelate was legitimately impeded.[32]

[28] C. 3, D. XCIII. [29] C. 4, D. XCIII.

[30] *Glossa Ordinaria,* ad c. 4, D. XCIII, s.v. *propinqui sunt.*

[31] *Corpus Iuris Civilis* (3 vols., Berolini, 1928-1929; Vol. II, *Codex Iustinianus* (quem Paulus Krueger recognovit et retractavit, ed. sterotypa 10., 1929), C. (7.33)12.

[32] *Glossa Ordinaria,* ad c. 4, D. XCIII, s.v. *praesententur.*

The concession was later incorporated in the Decretals of Gregory IX and expressed in more positive terms.[33]

The fact that the territory of a bishop's jurisdiction was quite distant from the Province of Rome constituted a legitimate reason that excused him from attendance at the Roman provincial council. The Glossator called attention to other decisions in which the handicap of distance was considered a valid excuse.[34]

Historical evidence points out that ecclesiastical authority decreed a similar consideration for those who were faced with hazardous travel when gathering for episcopal elections. For example, it was the custom in Spain that upon the death of a bishop all his fellow prelates of the various provinces of the country assembled to attend his obsequies, and thereupon notified the king of the necessity of electing a new bishop. Upon receiving the royal nomination, they proceeded to an election, and then waited for the king's approval of their office. The difficulty of travel during this era proved a great obstacle in the interchange of communications. Moreover, if after the election the bishops had adjourned while waiting for the king's confirmation, they then would have had to re-convene for the consecration of the one chosen. This would have meant a great inconvenience. Therefore, the bishops of Spain agreed that the Archbishop of Toledo should have the power of confirming and then consecrating the newly-elected bishops of any province in the country.[35]

A more specific determination was given to the expression *"de longinquo"* when the Glossator stated that the dioceses of the bishops were to be considered as being distant or remote if they lay outside of Italy. He substantiated this opinion by referring the reader to the IV General

[33] "Limina Apostolorum singulis annis, aut per me, aut per certum nuntium (meum) vistabo. . . ."—C. 4, X, *de iureiurando*, II, 24.

[34] *Glossa Ordinaria*, ad c. 4, D. XCIII, s.v. *de longinquo*.

[35] C. 25, D. LXIII; XII Council of Toledo (681), canon 6—Labbaeus-Cossartius, *Sacrosancta Concilia ad regiam editionem exacta* (17 vols. in 18, Parisiis, 1671-1672), VI, 1232.

Council of the Lateran (1215). Canon 4 of that Council was concerned with the election and confirmation of those who were chosen for the episcopacy. After stating in detail the requirements of the *"electi,"* the decree established that the newly chosen ones, if they were immediately subject to the Holy See, were to present themselves personally to the Pope for confirmation. If they were unable to fulfill this obligation in person, they were permitted to send a qualified representative with the pertinent information. The delegate was then given the letters of confirmation if no impediment existed. If, however, the validly elected bishops were *"valde remoti ultra Italiam,"* they were not to refrain from administering their dioceses during the interim, lest harm should befall the Church there.[36]

The Glossator of the *Decretum Gratiani* considered as *remoti* all bishops whose dioceses were more than a two days journey from Rome.[37] The glossators of the Gregorian Decretals taught that, although the boundaries of Italy were not everywhere equally distant from Rome, nevertheless the dioceses were to be deemed remote if it took a two and a half or a three days' journey to reach the Eternal City. That, he contended, had been established by custom.[38]

Permission for a bishop to remain absent from the Roman Councils could be contained in the certificate which he signed at the time of his consecration and the procedure which he was then to follow was explicitly set down. But unless such was the case, a bishop was not to forego attendance at these councils. If there was a sufficiently grave cause, the bishop was directed to send a legate, who was to accept in the bishop's name the decisions which the council established.[39]

It was the opinion of some of the Decretists that the

[36] C. 44, X, *de electione et electi potestate,* I, 6; Mansi, XXII, 1014.

[37] *Glossa Ordinaria,* ad c. 4, D. XCIII, s.v. *de longinquo.*

[38] *Glossa Ordinaria,* ad c. 44, X, *de electione et electi potestate,* I, 6, s.v. *ultra Italiam.*

[39] *Glossa Ordinaria,* ad c. 4, D. XCIII, s.v. *iuxta.*

word *"chirographum"* was to be understood as a letter that was to be sent to the Pope. Rufinus (†1190) was among those who espoused this opinion. He explained it in this manner: "Illi vero episcopi, qui sunt in provincia Romanae Ecclesiae vel ab ea consecrationem accipiunt, eam reverentiam debent papae, ut singulis annis ipsum visitent; *si autem de longinquo sunt, ei* (i.e., papae) *se per litteras commendent."*[40]

Stephen Tournai (1128-1203), however, pointed out a different intepretation: "... (chirographum) secundum quod a romana ecclesia impetraverunt et rescriptum meruerunt."[41]

Huguccio (†1210), on the other hand, seemed to draw a distinction between these interpretations when he wrote: "Iuxta chirographum suum, i.e., scriptum aut cautionem quam̃ fecerunt Apostolico in ordinatione sua, i.e., secundum quod per cautionem iuratoriam spoponderunt se facturo.... Ergo, et propinqui et longinqui tenentur hoc facere per se vel per legatos et litteras excusatorias, vel tantum per litteras excusatorias."[42]

As early as 1210, Alanus proposed the opinion that the delegate needed to have "letters" when he represented an absent bishop, as an indication of the fact that he had been duly authorized to act in that capacity.[43]

But in order to have a practical norm to follow when they were prevented from fulfilling the papal visitation personally, there were undoubtedly some prelates who used the interpretation of Rufinus. Perhaps Ioannes Teutonicus (†1245) in preparing the Gloss of the *Decretum*

[40] Rufinus, *Summa Decretorum,* p. 184.

[41] *Die Summa des Stephanus Tornacensis über das Decretum Gratiani* (ed. J. F. von Schulte, Giessen: Roth, 1891), p. 113 (hereafter cited as *Summa Decreti Gratiani*).

[42] Cf. J. Cottier, "Elements nouveaux des normes de la visité 'ad limina' et leur valeur juridique respective, des Décrétales au Concile de Trente," *Ephemerides Iuris Canonici* (Romae, 1945—), VIII (1952), 188, footnote (hereafter cited as Cottier).

[43] *Loc. cit.*

had such an opinion in mind when he wrote, "iuxta chirographum, expediri *per alias sufficit*."[44]

Relative to penalties for the non-observance of this law, Pope Hadrian I (772-795) was asked whether an accused prelate should suffer excommunication when he does not appear at the council after he had been properly summoned. When he signed his certificate at the time of his consecration, the bishop bound himself by an oath to perform the duty of visitation. The Holy Father replied that if the bishop was ill or otherwise seriously impeded, he should send a legate who would present the reason for his absence.[45]

But the ecclesiastical authorities did not hesitate to punish those who were lax in regard to this duty. It had been decreed by the Council of Agde (507), that, if a bishop when summoned by the metropolitan did not appear, he was to be deprived of the charity of his brother prelates and of communion with the Church until the next convocation of the bishops.[46] If such was the punishment for an unlawful absence from a gathering called by the Metropolitan, how much more so would the same punishment be applicable if a prelate neglected to attend a council convoked by the Sovereign Pontiff.

In consequence then, of the legislation of the Council of Rome, all bishops who lived within the province of Rome or were consecrated by or who received the pallium from the Pope were bound to attend the provincial councils held in the Eternal City, and while there to visit the tombs of the Apostles unless lawfully excused.

Historical evidence demonstrates that there were instances when obligatory attendance at these councils was not limited to that group of prelates. A letter (863) of Pope Nicholas I (858-867) to the Emperor Louis II (855-875) and to King Charles the Bald (843-877), reveals that the bishops of Germany and France were summoned to

[44] *Glossa Ordinaria*, ad c. 4, D. XCIII, s.v. *iuxta*.
[45] C. 1, C. V, q. 3; Mansi, XII, 907.
[46] *Glossa Ordinaria*, ad c. 4, D. XCIII, s.v. *canonicis*.

one of these councils. The Pope stressed the importance of these councils and expressed the desire of having at least a representative number of bishops of the empire attend.[47]

And Gregory VII (1073-1085), in a letter to the bishops of Lombary, spoke of the *general* character of the Roman Councils.[48]

The presence of foreign bishops for the consideration of affairs concerning the universal Church gave to the Roman Provincial Councils the appearance of general councils.[49]

Although there is no evidence that in these councils a report was demanded from or given by the attending bishops, the very presence of the latter as well as the desire of the popes that a representative number of bishops attend suggests that the councils provided the Pope with a source of valuable information regarding the affairs of the Church at large.

ARTICLE III. LEGISLATION CONTAINED IN THE DECRETALS OF GREGORY IX (1227-1241)

Section 1. Author of the Oath Whereby Bishops Obliged Themselves to the Visitation

In the centuries after the Council of Rome, it became customary for all bishops throughout the world, regardless of the source of their consecration, to journey to Rome, there to venerate the tombs of the Apostles Peter and Paul and to offer respect and obedience to the Sovereign Pontiff, while reporting to him on the condition of their dioceses. Moreover, by the eleventh century it had become

[47] *Monumenta Germaniae Historica, Epistolarum Tomus VI, Epistolae Karolini Aevi IV* (ed. Ernestus Perels, Berolini: apud Weidmannos, 1925), p. 309 (hereafter cited *MGH, Epp., VI*); Nicholas I, ep. 27—Mansi, XV, 290.

[48] *Monumenta Germaniae Historica, Gregorii VII Registrum,* Lib. I, ep. 43, *Epistolae Selectae,* Tom. II, fasc. I (ed. E. Casper, Berolini: apud Weidmannos, 1920), p. 66; JL, n. 4820.

[49] Thomassinus, Pars II, lib. III, cap. XLI, n. 3.

a practice for metropolitans also to come to the Eternal City in order to petition the Pope for the pallium.[50]

From the time of Gregory VII (1073-1085) there was abundant evidence that the *ad limina* visit—to which bishops and archbishops bound themselves under oath—was vigorously insisted upon. There was indication, too, that a report was demanded on these occasions. Gregory VII was a determined reformer of the clerical state and a defender of the Church's rights. His aim was to uphold ecclesiastical discipline and, regardless of personages, he required of all prelates the observance of this practice. That fact is apparent from an examination of his letters.[51]

Pope Paschal II (1099-1118) wrote to an Archbishop in Poland to remind him that the pallium was conferred only after the oath of fidelity and obedience had been personally rendered to the Supreme Pontiff.[52]

Pope Eugene III (1145-1153) wrote a letter to the people of Arras, France, and among other matters which he wished to bring to their attention mentioned the fact that the Bishop of Arras had journeyed to Rome and given a report of the conditions existing in the diocese, for which fact the Pope was grateful.[53]

Further proof of the established practice can be drawn from a note which Pope Hadrian IV (1154-1159) dispatched to Emperor Frederick I of Germany (1152-1190). The Holy Father rebuked him for the conditions existing in his country, and commanded him to revoke the edict which forbade ecclesiastical personages to make their *"debita visitatio"* to Rome.[54]

In like manner, Pope Innocent III (1198-1216) stressed

[50] Cappello, *De Visitatione*, I, 7.

[51] *MGH, Gregorii VII Registrum*, Lib. VI, ep. 30, *ibid.*, p. 443; Lib. VII, ep. 1, *ibid.*, p. 458; Lib. VII, ep. 13, *ibid.*, p. 477; Lib. VII, ep. 20, *ibid.*, p. 496. Cf. also JL, nn. 5121; 5135; 5153; 5163:

[52] *Epistolae Paschalis II*, ep. 6—Hardouin, VI B, 1768; Mansi, XX, 986.

[53] *Epistolae Papae Eugenii III*, ep. 558—*MPL*, CLXXX, 1575; ep. 560—*MPL*, CLXXX, 1579.

[54] *Epistolae Papae Adriani IV*, ep. 4—Hardouin, VII, 1337.

the importance of the obligation regarding the visit to be made to Rome.[55]

Pope Gregory IX (1227-1241), keenly aware that there was no uniformity in the observance of this law, and cognizant of the confusion and sometimes even contradictory interpretations given to the extant ecclesiastical legislation, decided that "for the good of the clergy and the laity alike, a general reordering of the Church's laws was needed for a more expeditious treatment of questions both in the Roman and diocesan curias. This work he entrusted to the illustrious Spanish Dominican, St. Raymond of Pennafort, directing him to form a new collection from all pre-existing compilations."[56]

In 1234, Pope Gregory IX by means of the Constitution *Lex pacificus* promulgated this collection as the official body of canon law. In preparing this collection of laws, St. Raymond followed the accepted procedure and divided the work into five books, the second of which he devoted to the subject of trials and judgments in the ecclesiastical courts. The twenty-fourth title of this section of the Decretals treats of oaths in general. In the fourth chapter was inserted the oath that imposed upon bishops the grave obligation of the *ad limina* visit. The last part of this oath read as follows: "Limina Apostolorum singulis annis aut per me aut per certum nuntium visitabo, nisi eorum absolvar licentia. Sic me Deus adiuvet et haec sancta Evangelia."[57]

Before the presentation of a historical and juridical analysis of this important text, there should be drawn a clear distinction between two obligations inherent in it: a) the obligation of taking the oath and b) the obligation resulting from it. In his recent article on the *ad limina* visit,

[55] *Epistolae Papae Innocentii III*, Lib. VII, ep. 124—*MPL*, CCXV, 295; Lib. XIII, ep. 123—*MPL*, CCVI, 312.

[56] Cicognani, *Canon Law* (2. ed., revised; Reprint, Westminster, Maryland: The Newman Press, 1949), p. 298 (hereafter cited as Cicognani).

[57] C. 4, X, *de iureiurando*, II, 24.

Julien Cottier made the observation that the promulgation of the duty of taking such a pledge was not an innovation. He stated that prior to 1234 there was something of a particular promulgation for each newly elected bishop inasmuch as the duty to take the oath was made known to him at the time he received notice of his appointment to the bishopric. Later, when Gregory IX promulgated his Decretals, the obligation of taking the oath was generally and officialy enforced.

Cottier further observed that, regarding the duties inherent in the oath once it was taken, these were of a special character, particular to each prelate. It is true, indeed, that Decretal law denfined these duties, but it did so only in a general way. The Apostolic See acknowledged extenuating circumstances in the case of each bishop. In such an instance the prelate who took the oath 'promulgated' as it were, for himself the various duties to which he was to be obliged.[58]

The rubric accompanying the text of this oath ascribes its authorship to a Pope Gregory, without further indentification, who addressed it to Peter a subdeacon, who was acting as his legate in Sicily. Because of this relative anonymity, commentators have differed in naming just which Pope Gregory was responsible for formulating the oath.

The oath was an important milestone in the historical development of the *ad limina* visit and report. Hence a correct identification of its author is necessary for determining at just what period the oath became obligatory.

It was an established practice in Spain during the seventh century that at the time of their consecration bishops would make a) *a profession of faith* and b) *a general promise* of observing the canons together with a pledge of loyalty to their superiors.[59]

The Spanish bishops, according to Thomassin (1619-

[58] "Elements nouveaux des normes de la visité 'ad limina' et leur valeur juridique respective, des Décrétales au Concile de Trente," p. 175.

[59] XI Council of Toledo (675), canon 10—Hardouin, III, 1028.

1695), were the first to make such an act of faith and obedience.[60]

It was St. Boniface (673-754) who solemnized with an oath the pledge of fidelity which he professed to Pope Gregory II (715-731).[61]

Prior to that time there is no evidence that *sacramenta* were attached to the promises of obedience and fidelity that were made by bishops to their metropolitans, or by bishops and metropolitans to the Pope.[62]

In the ninth and tenth centuries, the bishops continued the practice, however, of making a *profession of faith,* a pledge of unity and obedience to the Sovereign Pontiff and of the observance of his decrees. It was not until the eleventh century that an *oath* was added to those promises[63]

The initial historical evidence of such an oath was found in a canon of a Roman Council held in 1079. It was recorded there that Gregory VII demanded from the Archbishop of Aquileia not only a profession of canonical obedience but also an oath of fidelity that he would fulfill this allegiance. Pope Gregory chose to make this firm claim because of a schism which had affected many of the Italian and German bishops. In receiving them back into the Church, Gregory determined that the usual statement of loyalty should be strengthened with an oath.[64]

In the thirteenth century the Roman Pontiffs demanded an oath of fidelity a) from all bishops immediately subject to them, and b) from metropolitans who received the pallium from the Pope. The oath was to be taken according to

[60] *Vetus et Nova Ecclesiae Disciplina,* Pars II, lib. II, cap. 40, n. 6.

[61] *Monumeta Germania Historica, Epistolae Selectae, I, S. Bonifatii et Lullii Epistolae* (ed. M. Tangl, Berolini: Apud Weidmannos, 1916), n. 16.

[62] Catalanus, Pars I, tit. XIII, *de consecratione electi in episcopum,* cap. IX, n. 2.

[63] Van Espen, *Ius Ecclesiasticum Universum* (5 vols., Lovanii, 1753), Pars I, tit. II, *de consecratione episcoporum,* cap. 2, n. 3; Thomassinus, Pars II, lib. II, cap. 40.

[64] Council of Rome (1079)—Hardouin, VI, 1586.

the formula prescribed by Gregory VII. Moreover, metropolitans could demand the same oath from their suffragans.[65]

It can be determined from these historical evidences, therefore, that neither Gregory I (590-604), nor Gregory II (715-731), nor Gregory III (731-741), was the author of the *oath* found in the fourth chapter, *de iureiurando,* since such a *iuramentum* was not in existence at the time of their pontificates, nor was it a practice of the popes to insist upon one at the time of a bishop's consecration.

Although Gregory I dispatched several epistles to a papal legate named Peter (subdeacon), none of them contained the words of the disputed text.[66]

Hallier (1595-1659), however, wrote that "mihi sane videtur non incommode praedictum decretum *Gregorio secudo saltem ex parte* tribui posse." His contention was based on an oath by St. Boniface before Pope Gregory II at the time of the Saint's consecration.[67]

From a comparison of the texts containing the oaths involved in this matter, a) the oath of Boniface;[68] b) the oath as found in the Decretal;[69] and c) the oath demanded by Gregory VII,[70] it may be noted that the oath required by Gregory VII contained almost the exact words which were found in the Decretal text. The apparent discrepancy between "regalia S. Petri" of the Gregorian text and "regulas SS. Patrum" of the Decretals occurred, according to Gonzales-Tellez, in the transcription of the text. The Gregorian text was probably written, in abbreviated form,

[65] C. 13, X, *de maioritate et obedientia,* I, 33.

[66] Gonzalez-Tellez, *Commentaria Perpetua in Singulos Textus Quinque Librorum Decretalium Gregorii IX* (5 vols., Lugduni, 1673), Lib. II, tit. 24, cap. 12 (hereafter cited as *Commentaria*).

[67] *De sacris electionibus et ordinationibus ex antiquo et novo Ecclesiae usu* (3 vols., Romae: Mainardi, 1740), Tom. I, Pars I, Sect. VI, n. 2 (hereafter cited as *De sacris electionibus*).

[68] *MGH, Epistolae Selectae, I, S. Bonifatii et Lullii Epistolae,* n. 16.

[69] C. 4, X, *de iureiurando,* II, 24.

[70] *MGH, Gregorii VII Registrum,* Lib. VI, ep. 17 a, *Epistolae Selectae,* Tom. II, fasc. I, p. 428; JL, n. 5102.

such as "R.S.P.," i.e., "Regalia Sancti Petri," and the *compilatores collectionum* read that to be "regulas sanctorum Patrum." As an explanation of their words, they prefixed a cross to that phrase, emphasizing that the prelate taking the oath was bound to the prescriptions of the Pontiffs past and present. Moreover, for the letter "G" as found in the Gregorian text they placed the letter "C." Such an error, if it be that, could easily occur when it is remembered with what difficulty those ancient texts were read and transposed. As Gonzalez-Tellez pointed out, the presence of the letter "C" could have denoted that from the time of Celestine II (1143-1144) or Gelasius III (1191-1198) such a formula was used.[71]

Furthermore, if, as Hallier contended, Gregory II (715-731) was the author of the oath, it seems strange that Gregory VII (1073-1085), a great reform Pope, did not make use of it.

Regarding the question whether Gregory IX was the author of the oath, both Hallier and Gonzalez-Tellez denied that assumption. Each pointed out that the personal constitutions of Gregory IX (1227-1241), as they were cited in every volume of the Decretals, were invariably found in the last place of each title. Since Gregory IX was the Sovereign Pontiff who ordered the compilation of the Decretals, he gave precedence to the constitutions of those popes who were his predecessors. It is worthy of observation that Gregory VII was the author of chapters two and three of this title.[72]

The opinion of Gonzalez-Tellez, therefore, who named Gregory VII (1073-1085) as the proper author of this oath, appears to be strengthened by the most conclusive evidence. He is not alone, however, in this contention. Many others, principal among them being Pope Benedict XIV, shared a similar view.[73]

[71] Gonzalez-Tellez, *Commentaria,* Lib. II, tit. 24, cap. 12.

[72] Gonzalez-Tellez, *Commentaria,* Lib. II, tit. 24, cap. 12; Hallier, *De sacris electionibus,* Tom. I, Pars I, Sect. VI, p. 304.

[73] Benedictus XIV, *De Synodo Dioecesana,* Lib. XIII, cap. 6, n. 12;

Section 2. Interpretation of the Oath

The oath itself contained seven articles, which considered the duty of submission, obedience and fidelity that every bishop owed to the Apostolic See. The last article of the oath was specifically concerned with the duty incumbent upon every bishop to journey to Rome every year, fulfilling that duty either personally or through a properly recognized agent.

For a better understanding of that obligation, the text which incorporates mention of it, may be set down here verbatim. The exegesis will deal with the pertinent phrases.

> Limina Apostolorum singulis annis, aut per me, aut per certum nuntium (meum) visitabo, nisi eroum absolvar licentia. Sic me Deus adiuvet de haec sancta Evangelica.[74]

Historical evidence indicates no important distinction regarding the manner in which prelates of different rank were to take this oath. Cottier, however, mentions the procedure established for those prelates who had been consecrated at the Roman Curia. Those bishops, he said, were not bound to take the oath on the very day of their consecration, but it was necessary that this pledge be made before they left the Apostolic See. Generally it was made on the day of the Consistory. At the end of the Consistory, two of the Cardinal Deacons escorted the bishop to an altar especially prepared for the purpose and occasion, and there received the oath of fealty in the name of the Sovereign Pontiff. If the newly consecrated prelate did not take the oath at that time, he was not permitted to leave the Curia.[75] That was essentially the traditional procedure, and it remained in effect until Leo X (1513-1521) decreed an official ceremonial.[76]

Lucidi, I, 11; Coronata, I, n. 399; Cappello, *De Visitatione,* I, 8; Cicognani, p. 301.

[74] C. 4, X, *de iureiurando,* II, 24.

[75] Cottier, p. 175.

[76] "... quicumque ... (prelatus) ... promotus fuerit et ipse praesens in Romana Curia existiterit..., debeat... in manibus dilecti filii nostri prioris diaconorum S. R. E. cardinalium pro tempore existentis,

For those prelates who received their consecration or benediction outside the Roman Curia by means of a mandate from the Pope, the following procedure was in force. The formula of the oath was enclosed in the mandate of appointment. The ceremony then was similar to the one already described above, inasmuch as the bishop pledged his loyalty and fidelity before a delegate of the Pope. The delegate then reported the fulfillment of his office with the '*formula iuramenti*' properly signed and sealed.[77]

Limina Apostolorum . . . visitabo

Canonists have almost always unanimously concurred in understanding the phrase, "*visitabo liminum SS. Apostolorum,*" as pointing to three distinct acts, namely, the visiting of the basilicas of the Holy Apostles Peter and Paul, the showing of reverence and obedience to the Holy Father, and finally the presenting of the report concerning the status of the diocese.

But in the thirteenth century, in view of the extant circumstances of an extraordinary nature, a most important question arose in regard to this matter: what was to be understood by "*limina Apostolorum*" when the Pope was not in Rome. When Innocent IV (1243-1254) remained in Lyons for several years—from 1245 to 1251[78]—it was asked, whither—to Rome or to Lyons—were the prelates to journey in order to fulfill their *ad limina* visit.

In his Commentary of the Decretals, Innocent IV presented his answer to this problem. The "*Liminum Apostolorum visitatio*" was to take place, he wrote, where the Pope was in residence.[79]

. . . (infra mensem) . . . vocato uno dictis ex ceremoniarum magistris, iuxta consuetudinem hactenus servatam . . . iuramentum . . . praestare." —*Bullarum Diplomatum et Privilegiorum Sanctorum Romanorum Pontificum Taurinensis Editio* (24 vols. et Appendix, Augustae Taurinorum, 1857-1872), V, p. 684, § 2 (hereafter cited as *BRT*).

77 Cottier, p. 177.

78 Hughes, *A History of the Church* (3 vols., New York: Sheed and Ward, Inc., 1934, 1935, 1947), I, 442-444.

79 "Apostolorum autem limina ibi esse intelliguntur ubi papa est."

That interpretation of the words *"Limina Apostolorum visitatio"* has been followed by all noteworthy canonists. More specifically, it was determined that the place of the Pope's residence was to be understood as the location of his Court, even though the Sovereign Pontiff was temporarily absent.[80]

Hostiensis furnished a most lucid interpretation regarding the meaning of *"limina apostolorum."* The tombs of the Apostles Peter and Paul, so he claimed, were to be understood as the Roman Curia, because Rome was where the Pope was! And from this fact, so he argued, it was evident that, where the Pope was, there also the Apostles were understood to be. This conclusion was valid when one considered the words *"nisi eorum absolvar licentia."* The only logical explanation of the words *"eorum licentia"* was that of a special privilege granted by the Pope as present at the tombs of the Apostles, enjoying the same authority as the Apostles—being their legitimate successor, and therefore acting in their stead.[81]

Limina Apostolorum *singulis annis* . . . visitabo

Although the oath itself demanded an annual visitation, the fact that they were a great distance from Rome often permitted bishops to seek and obtain indults that extended the time in which it was required to make the visit. But it seems that up to about the middle of the thirteenth century there were only three categories of prelates as far as this matter was concerned, viz., the *citramontani,* the *ultarmontani* and the *ultramarini,* who respectively were obliged to visit the Apostolic See every year, every second

—Innocentius IV, *In Quinque Libros Decretalium Commentaria* (Venetiis, 1570), Lib. II, XXIV, *de iureiurando,* cap. 4.

[80] C. 4, D. XCIII: "Illi vero episcopi . . . eam reverentiam debent papae ut singulis annis ipsum visitent . . ."—Rufinus, *Summa Decretorum,* p. 184: ". . . quidam sunt episcopi . . . debent visitare romanam ecclesiam."—Stephanus Tornacensis, *Summa Decreti Gratiani,* p. 112.

[81] Hostiensis (Henricus de Segusio), *Commentaria in Quinque Decretalium Libros* (5 vols., Venetiis, 1581), Lib. II, tit. XXIV, *de iureiurando,* cap. 4, n. 8 (hereafter cited as *Commentaria*).

year, or every third or fifth year. Later the English and Spanish prelates were permitted to make the *ad limina* visit every third year. It seems that the maximum time limit allowed never exceeded ten years.

In commenting on this section of the Decretal, Hostensis described a similar arrangement: "Iuxta hoc autem in citra montanis locum habet regulariter. Ultra montanis vero mare non transeuntes iurant singulis bienniis; ultra marini autem singulis trienniis, et sic consideratur locorum distantia."[82]

In the Decretal itself, the Glossator made the notation that, according to the document which the bishop signed at the time of his consecration, he might be permitted to make the journey less frequently because of the factor of distance and other extenuating circumstances.[83]

This interpretation was in accord with that given by almost all Decretists to a parallel passage in Gratian.[84]

Bishops and archbishops alike who were immediately subject to the Pope by reason of their consecration or reception of the pallium, whether at the hands of the Pope himself or through a papal mandate, were considered bound by the law. Ioannes Andreae (1272-1348) made a similar observation: prelates were bound if they had received their confirmation, consecration or the pallium from the Sovereign Pontiff.[85]

> "Limina Apostolorum singulis annis, aut *per me aut per certum nuntium (meum)* visitabo."

A. *Per Me*

Except for extraordinary circumstances, there was no reason why the time determined for a prelate's visit to

[82] *Commentaria,* Lib. II, tit. XXIV, *de iureiurando,* cap. 4, n. 8.

[83] *Glossa Ordinaria,* c. 4, X, *de iureiurando,* II, 24, s.v. *singulis annis.*

[84] *Glossa Ordinaria,* c. 4, D. XCIII, s.v. *per chirographum;* cf. pp. 15-19.

[85] *In Quinque Decretalium Libros Novella Commentaria* (5 vols., Venetiis, 1581), Lib. II, tit. XXIV, *de iureiurando,* cap. 4, p. 184 (hereafter cited as Ioannes Andreae).

the Holy See should be extended. Such an assumption was based on the fact that each prelate could discharge his duty either personally or, if he was impeded, through a legitimate representative. As has been noted above, a bishop was not to forego attendance at the council unless he was prevented from fulfilling that obligation by a sufficiently grave excuse. In such an instance, the bishop was directed to send a legate, who would accept in his name the decisions made in the Council.[86]

Then, in the IV General Council of the Lateran (1215), it was decided that the prelates were to be urged to make at least the *first visit personally,* so that thereby they might obtain confirmation of their office.[87]

B. *Per Certum Nuntium (Meum)*

With the progress of time, the *ad limina* visit came more and more to be made by delegates of the bishops. Even those prelates whose dioceses lay relatively near to Rome assigned this duty to a representative.

Furthermore, there arose the practice of having agents who lived at the Roman Curia fulfill that obligation. That custom had developed from the fact that in some manuscripts of the Decretals the prononun *"meum"* was omitted from the phrase *"per certum nuntium meum."* As a result, just as the manuscripts were divided between those in which the word *"meum"* was mentioned and those in which it was not, so also the prelates were divided between those who actually *sent* delegates *"in latere"* as it were, and those who *delegated agents living in Rome* to carry out their visitation.[88]

It was not necessary that the delegate or agent possess any particular dignity in order to qualify for this office. He could be a canon or a monk, a deacon or a subdeacon,

[86] C. 9, D. XVIII.

[87] C. 44, X, *de electione et electi potestate,* I, 6; Mansi, XXII, 1014.

[88] Cf. c. 4, X, *de iureiurando,* II, 24. In the Richter-Friedberg edition of the *Corpus Iuris Canonici* a footnote indicates the absence of the pronoun *"meum"* in the *Collect. Decret. Bamberg.*

a cleric or a layman, as long as he could function as a secretary.[89]

It was the opinion of Hostiensis and of other commentators of the thirteenth and fourteenth centuries that the delegate was to present credentials in attestation of the authenticity of his mandate, and also a *"relatio"* concerning the religious condition of the Church which he was deputed to represent.[90]

Cottier proposed the hypothesis that the practice whereby the procurator was obliged to submit a *"relatio"* had its origin in the interpretation which canonists gave to canon 4 of the Council of Rome (743). He cited the various and sometimes conflicting explanations of the word *"chirographum"* in c. 4, D. XCIII.[91]

The interpretation of Hostiensis and of other Decretalists, however, seems more in conformity with the canonical tradition, which demanded that *all* bishops submit a report to the Apostolic See. There is no historical evidence to indicate that the *relatio* was limited to an *oral* report made at the time of the visitatio *ad limina.* On the contrary, as

[89] Cottier, p. 184.

[90] *Certum nuntium*—"propter hoc litteris statum ecclesiae continentibus specialiter destinatum,"—Hostiensis, *Commentaria,* Lib II, tit. XXIV *de iureiurando,* cap. 4, n. 8, p. 126; Ioannes Andreae, Lib. II, tit. XXIV, *de iureiurando,* cap. 4, p. 184; Panormitanus, *Commentaria in Quinque Libros Decretalium* (5 vols. in 7, Venetiis, 1588), Lib. II, tit. XXIV, *de iureiurando,* cap. 4.

[91] "Si autem aliqui de longinquo sunt, se ei i.e., Papae, per litteras comendent."—Rufinus, *Summa Decretorum,* p. 184; "(chirographum) secundum quod a romana ecclesia impetraverunt et rescriptum meruerunt."—Stephanus Tornacensis, *Summa Decreti Gratiani,* p. 113; "iuxta chirographum, i.e., scriptum aut cautionem quam fecerunt Apostolico in ordinatione sua, i.e., secundum quod per cautionem iuratoriam spoponderunt se facturos.—Ergo, et propingui et longinqui tenentur hoc facere per se, vel per legatos et litteras excusatorias, vel tantum per litteras excusatorias."—(quoted by Cottier in his article on p. 188). Cottier mentioned in the same place that it was the opinion of the Decretalist Alanus in 1210 that the delegate must have letters testifying to the authenticity of his mandate. From a study of these opinions, Cottier drew the inference that only those bishops were to submit a written report who fulfilled their obligation *per alium.*

has been pointed out above, the Popes on numerous occasions wrote letters of commendation or rebuke to bishops for having complied with or neglected the duty of preparing and drawing up written reports of their churches.[92]

> "Limina Apostolorum singulis annis, aut per me, aut per certum nuntium (meum) visitabo, *nisi eorum absolvar licentia.*"

The Decretalists did not agree in their interpretation of the phrase "*eorum licentia*" contained in the clause "*nisi eorum absolvar licentia.*" As was noted in reference to the correct meaning of "*Limina Apostolorum,*" the only logical explanation that could be given to these words was the one that pointed to a special privilege granted by the Pope, the Sovereign Pontiff, who, present at the tombs of the Apostles and as their legitimate successor, acted in their place.[93]

In this regard, the reader should again recall the distinction made earlier between the obligation of taking the oath and the obligation resulting from the oath once it had been taken. It is noteworthy that none of the texts furnish any indication of a complete abrogation of the obligation of taking the oath as far as prelates immediately subject to the Pope were concerned. That is a valuable indication of the seriousness and importance with which the Apostolic See considered this law. It is true, however, that there was something of a 'negative dispensation' that favored certain prelates in their special status, e.g., distance from Rome.

There was less difficulty in obtaining a dispensation from the obligation resulting from the oath. That was true because, although the prelate was dispensed on some particular occasion, there was still present the possibility of his fulfilling the duty periodically under better circumstances, and in that way the religious significance of the oath and its importance would be heeded. This obligation, though

[92] Cf. *supra*, pp. 7, 10, 21-23.

[93] Hostiensis, *Commentaria*, Lib. II, tit. XXIV, *de iureiurando*, cap. 4, n. 8, p. 126.

it was established for the benefit of the visible unity of the Church, could become non-performable by some particular bishop in varying circumstances either because its fulfillment stood in the way of some greater good (e.g., by not observing the law the prelate could better watch over his spiritual flock in some crisis) or because its fulfillment actually gave rise to something evil (e.g., the serious illness of an infirm bishop would be aggravated by his journey to Rome).[94]

A prelate could not presume, however, to dispense himself from these obligations. Rather, it was necessary that he present his application, based on a sufficient motive, to the proper authorities. This was required because of the sacred character of the oath. The assumed obligation was a grave one because it had been taken under oath, and therefore postulated a proportionately grave excuse for any dispensation from its fulfillment. Such a decision had to be made by some one other than the person seeking the dispensation.

The papal registers furnished a listing of some of the principal causes that were deemed acceptable. These causes could be of a public character or private, temporary or permanent. Among the more common public causes were war, local economic stress or straitened conditions, interference from the civil authority. Great distance, illness, poverty, the greater good to be obtained by a prelate's remaining in a newly occupied see—these could be listed among the private extenuating circumstances that could excuse one from the observance of the papal visitation.[95]

The power to dispense from this oath was the exclusive right of the Pope. St. Thomas listed it among the "major oaths" reserved to the discretionary power of the Sovereign Pontiff.[96]

Therefore, while a dispensation from other formal

[94] *Ibid.*, n. 9; Cottier, p. 195.

[95] Cottier, p. 196.

[96] *Summa Theologica* (3 vols., Taurini-Romae: Marietti, 1948), IIa IIae, q. 88, art. 12, ad 3.

pledges could be given by superiors in particular circumstances, a dispensation from this oath could be granted only by the Supreme Pontiff. Since it was the Pope who obligated the prelates to the duty of making the visitation and of submitting the report, he and only he could grant a relaxation of it, either directly or indirectly .

Moreover, as the properly chosen and valid successor of St. Peter, the reigning Pope possessed the authority to grant a dispensation from an oath made to any of his predecessors.[97]

The Pope could of course entrust this office to another by reason of the plenitude of his power. The rule of Boniface VIII, as just quoted in the footnote, certainly remained applicable. In principle, however, it was the Sovereign Pontiff and he alone who was capable of dispensing *"iure proprio."*[98]

Section 3. Law Regarding Metropolitans

The canonical interpretation which was given to the words *"nullo medio"* of canon 4 of the Council of Rome (743), made metropolitans also answerable to the prescriptions of the law of visitation. Inasmuch as the Pope was the sole ecclesiastical superior of a metropolitan, and particularly of a metropolitan who had received either his consecration and/or the pallium from the Pope himself, it was for these reasons that the metropolitan was regarded as being immediately subject (*nullo medio*) to the Sovereign Pontiff.[99]

By the eleventh century it was an accepted practice for metropolitans to journey to Rome and to petition the Pope for the pallium, and while there to perform the visitation.

This is evidenced in a letter written by Pope Paschal II (1099-1118) to an Archbishop in Poland who had refused to take the oath obligating him to the *visitatio ad limina.*

[97] Reg. 68, R. J.., in VI°: "Potest quis per alium, quod potest facere per seipsum;" St. Thomas, *Summa Theologica,* IIa, q. 72, art. II, ad I.

[98] Cottier, p. 198.

[99] Ioannes Andreae, Lib. II, tit. XXIV, *de iureiurando,* cap. 4, p. 184.

The Holy Father reminded the recalcitrant prelate that all the metropolitans of the Church took the oath and made the visit to the Eternal City. Moreover, some metropolitans whose provinces were farther distant from Rome than Poland, had taken the oath and had visited the tombs of the Apostles and paid their respect to the Pope—not only every third year (as they were permitted to do because of the distance), but every year.[100]

Innocent III (1198-1216) wrote a letter to the Patriarch of Antioch, who had neglected the duty of visiting the Eternal City because of alleged impediments. The Pope accepted the excuses offered, but advised the prelate that in the future he should perform the obligation as his predecessors had done.[101]

The practice of visiting the tombs of the Apostles was definitely established when the obligation of petitioning the Pope for the pallium was determined. The decretal legislation of Gregory IX (1227-1241) demonstrated in a clear fashion the procedure which the Apostolic See followed in this matter. The pallium was not given to any newly appointed archbishop unless he first took the oath of fidelity and obedience and promised to visit the tombs of the Apostles at designated intervals.[102]

Ioannes Andreae wrote that the duty of visitation was to be performed by those who had received *confirmation* (i.e., of their office), *consecration* or the *pallium* from the Pope.[103]

When Alexander IV (1254-1261) assumed the throne of Peter, he learned that some prelates had applied for and had obtained special indults exempting them from the prescribed journey to the tombs of the Apostles. The relaxa-

[100] Epistolae Paschalis II, ep. 6—Hardouin, VI B, 1768; Mansi, XX, 986; Augustinus, *Antiquae Decretalium Collectiones Commentariis et Emendationibus Illustratae* (Parisiis, 1621), c. 4, X, *de electione et electi potestate*, I, 6.

[101] Cf. Benedictus XIV, *De Synodo Dioecesana*, lib. XIII, cap. 6, n. 12; Lucidi, I, 12.

[102] C. 4, X, *de electione et electi potestate*, I, 6.

[103] *Commentaria*, Lib. II, tit. XXIV, *de iureiurando*, cap. 4, p. 184.

tion of the law had been made during the reign of Innocent IV (1243-1254), and a renewal of the indult was sought from Pope Alexander. In his Constitution *Importuno nimis* (1257), the Holy Father revoked all such privileges.[104]

Thus it is evident that as early as 1257 (and from the tenor of the Pope's declaration, even before) the *ad limina* visit was recognized as a serious duty which PATRIARCHS, ARCHBISHOPS, BISHOPS, ABBOTS AND OTHER PRELATES OF THE CHURCH had to obey. When it is remembered that the canonical interpretation of that obligation looked beyond the mere visit to the tomb of the Apostles, it is quite reasonable to assume that the visiting prelates in performing their acts of reverence and obedience to the Sovereign Pontiff, also presented to him a report on the status of the churches under their direction.

[104] *BRT*, III, 652.

CHAPTER II

LEGISLATION FROM POPE SIXTUS V (1585-1590) TO THE CODE

ARTICLE I. THE CONSTITUTION *Romanus Pontifex* (1585)

Section 1. Importance of the Law of Visitation and Report

When Sixtus V (1585-1590) ascended the throne of St. Peter, it was a most critical period in the history of the Church. It was a time of needed reform and Catholic restoration. The Protestant Revolt had spread throughout almost every country of Europe. The heretical teachings promoted by Hus (1373-1415), Zwingli (1484-1531), Calvin (1509-1564), Henry VIII (1491-1547) and especially Luther (1483-1546) had caused serious defections in Bohemia, Hungary and Transylvania, Denmark, Norway and Sweden, Switzerland, France England, Scotland and Germany.

The new Sovereign Pontiff was confronted with a grave crisis in France, one of great importance to the whole future of Europe—the saving of the Catholic Faith so seriously threatened by Calvinism, and the preservation of France as a powerful and independent state.[1] Furthermore, the threat of Spanish Caesaro-papism appeared all the more imminent.[2]

Because of his eminent position, Sixtus V had to declare a positive policy on these important matters. His piety, fearlessness, skill and zeal enabled Sixtus to do so, and as a result he was to be known in the history of the Popes as the savior not only of the independence of France but also of the liberties and independence of the papacy.

[1] Pastor, *History of the Popes* (40 vols., 1891-1953; Vol XXI, ed. by R. F. Kerr, St. Louis: B. Herder Book Co., 1932), XXI, 262 (hereafter cited as Pastor.

[2] *Ibid.*, XXI, 340.

Sixtus V, like his predecessor Gregory VII (1073-1085), can be truly classified as a reform Pope. Wherever he could, he carried on the work of reform and Catholic restoration, seeking to save what still could be saved, and striving to recover lost ground. His principal intent was to effect a closer union between the universal Church and the Papacy. This was to be the basis of his reform movement. A matter of principal concern, therefore, was the renewal of the almost forgotten practice of bishops journeying to Rome at stated intervals to inform the Holy Father of the status of their dioceses and, while in the Eternal City, to make a pilgrimage to the tombs of the Apostles Peter and Paul.[3]

This custom had fallen into disuse after the disturbance of the great schism (1378-1418). How important and necessary Sixtus V considered this practice can be well understood when attention is given to the fact that he was enthroned as Sovereign Pontiff on May 1st, and on December 20th of that same year promulgated his celebrated Constitution *Romanus Pontifex.* This official pronouncement of the new Pope concerned a matter the fulfillment of which was essential to the success of his reform program. Briefly, the Constitution decreed that thenceforth all bishops, archbishops, primates and patriarchs should, at the time of their consecration, their reception of the pallium, or their transfer to another jurisdiction, promise under oath that they would personally or through others visit the tombs of the Apostles and also submit to the Pope an account of the condition of their dioceses. This was to be done at defined intervals.[4]

Addressing his message to the hierarchy of the world, Sixtus began with a statement of the supreme authority of the Roman Pontiff over all bishops and of the obvious usefulness of a regular system of information. It was his duty as Peter's successor to demonstrate paternal care and solicitude towards all of Christ's flock. To make that bur-

[3] *Ibid.*, XXI, 5.

[4] Sixtus V, const. *Romanus Pontifex,* 20 dec. 1585, § 4—*Fontes,* n. 156

den lighter, the Pope pointed out, he had to depend upon the assistance of his brother bishops. It would be from them that he, as Supreme Pastor, would learn of the needs of the flocks everywhere committed to their care. And then, cognizant of their spiritual ills and defects, he could prescribe the proper remedies.[5]

The bishops were reminded that a neglect of so salutary a custom had brought harm not only to their own souls but to their dioceses as well. It was to just such a disregard of ecclesiastical duties that Sixtus attributed in part the origin and spread of the prevalent heretical doctrines. Now a renewal of the law was intended to give the Pope exact information as to the religious conditions of all nations, and thus to make possible a more practical and well informed intervention in every adverse religious development. Moreover, as a result of this legislation, the bishops themselves would necessarily keep a closer watch over the spiritual welfare of their subjects and at the same time be inspired to a keener sense of duty.[6]

The purpose and the importance of the legislation was obvious. It would bring bishops into a more intimate relationship with their supreme head, and also foster a deeper and more uniform transformation of religious conditions in accordance with the Tridentine decrees.[7]

The very words which Sixtus V used to impose the duty, "*Iubemus igitur in virtute sanctae obedientiae,*"[8] the severe penalties threatened for its non-observance,[9] the unanimous teaching of the authors, the fact that the prelates obligated themselves by taking an oath[10]—all these were indications of the gravity of the obligation.

[5] Sixtus V, const. *Romanus Pontifex*, 20 dec. 1585—*Fontes*, n. 156.
[6] Sixtus V, *ibid.*, § 3.
[7] Pastor, *History of the Popes*, XXI, 135.
[8] Sixtus V, const. *Romanus Pontifex*, 20 dec. 1585, § 7—*Fontes*, n. 156.
[9] *Ibid.*, § 8—*Fontes*, n. 156.
[10] *Ibid.*, § 3—*Fontes*, n. 156.

Section 2. The Oath Taken by Bishops at the Time of Their Consecration

To impress upon his brother bishops the seriousness of the duty they were asked to assume, Sixtus V ordained as positive law that all patriarchs, primates, archbishops and bishops were to take an oath affirming that they woud make an official visit and report to the Holy See on the administration of their dioceses at designated times. This oath was to be made before the prelates received their consecration, or, if already consecrated, *before* they received the pallium as an archbishop, or, if transferred to another see, *before* they undertook the rule and administration of the new diocese.[11]

The bishops took the oath according to a formula described in a book of the Apostolic Chancery. After swearing that they would faithfully perform the various duties and obligations of their episcopal office, the prelates solemnly promised to visit the Holy See and submit a report at the times determined by the law.[12]

If the bishop-elect, the newly chosen archbishop, or the transferred prelate was a member of the Papal Curia or was present in Rome, the oath was to be administered by the senior Cardinal Deacon, On the other hand, if the consecration, the reception of the pallium, or the transfer was to take place outside the Eternal City, the oath was to be made in the hands of the dignitary chosen by the Holy See to perform that duty.[13]

Section 3. Time Prescribed for the Making of the Visit and Report

Many phases of this law were in operation a number of centuries before the reign of Sixtus V. This has been determined. What this Pontiff accomplished, however, was to provide that the report might be made with becom-

[11] *Loc. cit.*

[12] Catalanus, Pars I, tit, XIII, *de consecratione electi in episcopum,* cap. VIII.

[13] *Loc. cit.*

ing uniformity and regularity, and that it might not become too great an inconvenience for ordinaries living at a distance from Italy. For that reason Sixtus established a definite time for performing these duties—every three, four, five or ten years. The periods were not common to all; they were determined and allotted to the bishops of the world according to the country in which they held their jurisdiction.

The computation of time was arranged, therefore, according to the country or region in which the particular diocese was located, and the periods were to *begin* at the time of the bishop's consecration, reception of the pallium, or transfer to another diocese.[14]

Those prelates who already had been consecrated, or had received the pallium, or had been transferred to another see, were subject to the prescriptions of the Constitution from the date of its publication, December 20, 1585.[15]

In regard to the newly appointed bishops, the Constitution decreed that the time periods began from the time of their consecration, of their reception of the pallium, or of their transfer. The Sacred Congregation of the Council interpreted this to mean, *not* that the *time of computation* of the triennium, etc., was to be determined from the very day of consecration, etc., but rather that as soon as a prelate was consecrated, or had received the pallium, or was transferred, there *began for him the obligation* that entailed the making of the visit and report.[16]

[14] Sixtus V, const. *Romanus Pontifex,* 20 dec. 1585, n. 6—*Fontes,* n. 156; S.C.C., *in Montis Alti,* 1584; S.C.C. *in Carpentoracten.,* 19 febr. 1788—Pallottini, *Collectio Omnium Conclusionum et Resolutionum* (17 vols., Romae, 1868-1893), s.v. *Episcopus,* IX, nn. 36-40 (hereafter cited as Pallottini).

[15] Sixtus V, const. *Romanus Pontifex,* 20 dec. 1585, § 7—*Fontes,* n. 156.

[16] Fagnanus, tit. XXIV, *de iureiurando,* nn. 37, 38; S. C. de Prop. Fide, instr. 1 iun. 1877, nn. 5-9—*Collectanea S. Congregationis de Propaganda Fide* (2 vols., Romae: Typographia Polyglotta S. C. de Propaganda Fide, 1907)—n. 1472 (hereafter cited as *Collectanea*); S. C. *in Montis Alti,* 1594—Pallottini, s.v. *Episcopus,* IX, n. 40.

In the event a bishop died or was removed from office and had not fulfilled the prescriptions of this law, his successor became bound to do so within the period assigned for his predecessor. This did not mean, however, that the succeeding prelate had to supply for all the visits and reports neglected by his predecessor; the new incumbent had simply to supply for the visit and report falling due in the current period. Thus, if a bishop had been consecrated on May 1, 1591, within the third year of the second triennium, and his predecessor had not conformed to the regulation of the Constitution, then the new Ordinary was bound to do so before December 20, 1591.[17]

If the remainder of the current period proved insufficient for the bishop to prepare a satisfactory report and to make his visit to Rome, he could ask for an extension of time from the Sacred Congregation of the Council.[18]

Although the Constitution did not explicitly indicate the exact year during the triennium, quadriennium, etc., in which the report and visit were to be made, nevertheless the fulfillment of the obligation could not be approached indiscriminately. Rather, it was the wish of the Apostolic See that the obligation be fulfilled in the *last year* of the period assigned. Otherwise, if it had been permissible to perform the visit at any period of time within the designated number of years, a bishop could have made his report and visit in the first year of one period, and then have waited until the last year of the next period before journeying to Rome again. This would not have been in keeping with the words of the Constitution, nor would it have suited the purpose for which the Pope promulgated the Constitution.[19]

Section 4. The "Ad Limina" Visit and Presentation of the Report

The prescriptions of the Constitution obliged bishops,

[17] Fagnanus, *ibid.*, n. 47; Lucidi, I, 36.
[18] Fagnanus, *ibid.*, n. 48; Lucidi, *loc cit.*
[19] Fagnanus, *ibid.*, n. 50.

archbishops, primates and patriarchs to the performance of a threefold duty: a visitation of the tombs of the Apostles Peter and Paul, who had consecrated the city with their blood; a personal visit to the Sovereign Pontiff, as a gesture of obedience and reverence; the submission of a report concerning their entire pastoral office and embracing all the matters pertinent to the care of their churches.

The first act was performed when the bishops paid a personal visit to the Basilicas of St. Peter and of St. Paul (Via Ostiense), and humbly venerated the tombs of the blessed Apostles. This visitation was not to be interpreted as referring to the city of Rome in general, or to the subsequent visit paid to the Holy Father. Bishops were to perform this pilgrimage as an act of honor to their bishop predecessors—Christ's personally chosen ones—who symbolized the rock of faith and source of the entire priestly unity.[20]

The purpose, however, of the visit to Rome was not only this pious pilgrimage. It was especially an occasion when the bishop manifested his obedience and submission to Peter's successor, the Holy Father, and informed him in a general way of the condition of his diocese. Sixtus V pointed out the evils which the Church had suffered when this duty had been neglected. The motivating cause which prompted Sixtus to publish his Constitution, and therefore the real purpose of the *ad limina* visit, was consolidation of the primacy of the Papacy. This he proposed to accomplish by demanding that all bishops come to the Apostolic See and apprise the Holy Father regarding the administration of their dioceses. The fulfillment of these directions would not only give rise to a greater bond of unity between the Supreme Pontiff and the Episcopacy, but would also enable the Chief Pastor to better procure the salvation of souls. It was absolutely necessary, however, that the Holy Father be well informed concerning the state of every diocese. This, it seems, was the keynote of the Sixtine

[20] Sixtus V, const. *Romanus Pontifex*, 20 dec. 1585, § 1—*Fontes*, n. 156; Fagnanus, tit. XXIV, *de iureiurando*, n. 62.

Constitution, and the underlying reason for the reports to be made, both verbal and written.[21]

The third act of the *ad limina* visit was satisfied when the bishop made his report, both orally and in writing to the Sacred Congregation of the Council. This report was concerned with both the material and the formal (spiritual) aspects of his diocese.[22]

Since this was the written record of the bishop's administration, and, as was noted above, such was the information desired by the Sovereign Pontiff, Catalani referred to this part of the visit as the chief scope of the visitation, basing his conclusion on the *stylus curiae,* which acted in conformity with the Sixtine Constitution.[23]

In his Constitution, Sixtus decreed, but only in a general way, that bishops were to submit a report "de toto eorum pastorali officio deque rebus omnibus ad ipsarum, quibus praesunt, ecclesiarum statum, ad cleri, et populi disciplinam, animarum denique, illorum fidei creditae sunt, salutem quovis modo pertinentibus. . . .[24]

In 1587, in his Constitution *Immensa aeterni Dei,* Sixtus V established a more specific discipline in this regard by providing that the Sacred Congregation of the Council was to receive the prelates who came to Rome to give an account of their pastoral office. This Congregation was equitably and justly to decide the matters which fell within the scope of its competence, but was to refer the more difficult affairs to the Pope. These Cardinals had been empowered by the Holy Father with the faculty of interpreting any doubts or difficulties concerning the enactments of the Council of Trent. Sixtus directed, therefore, that it was part of their duty to question bishops about the moral status of their clergy and people, concerning the observance of

[21] Sixtus V, *loc. cit.*

[22] Fagnanus, tit. XXIV, *de iureiurando,* n. 72.

[23] *Pontificale Romanum,* Pars I, tit. XIII, *de consecratione electi in episcopum,* cap. IX, n. 13.

[24] Sixtus V, const. *Romanus Pontifex,* 20 dec. 1585, § 3—*Fontes,* n. 156.

the Tridentine decrees, especially as to residence, regarding the pious customs that flourished in the diocese.[25]

Fagnani (1588-1678) was the first one to draw up a formula or questionnaire which indicated specifically in what manner and on what points the bishops were to prepare their reports. This formula did not, however, enjoy the authority of law, but it did serve as an invaluable aid to the prelates themselves, and also to Fagnani in his capacity of Secretary of the Congregation.[26]

The part of the report to which he referred as the *material* part Fagnani understood as that which concerned places, such as the cities, the suburban areas and rural districts. It related also to the cathedral, collegiate, parochial, and other churches and oratories. A report was to be made about the monasteries of both men and women, and regarding the hospitals, shrines, colleges, confraternities and other pious places situated in the see city and throughout the diocese, along with a mention of their location. The report also was to describe the type of church architecture, to list the decorations and furnishings and to indicate the number of persons and ministers. The *praxis curiae* demanded that the bishops submit a detailed report of this type at the time of their first visitation. In subsequent visits, in regard to the material status, they were obliged to note simply what had been added, subtracted or changed with reference to the previous report.[27]

The formal status of the diocese which, as Fagnani declared, was to be the primary concern of the prelates, had reference principally to the pastoral office and to all those matters which pertained to the ruling of the churches over which the bishops presided, and which contributed to the welfare of souls. Specifically, the bishops were to report whether they had celebrated a diocesan synod every year,

[25] Sixtus V, const. *Immensa aeterni Dei,* 22 ian. 1588—*BRT*, VIII, 991, 992.

[26] Van Espen, *Ius Ecclesiasticum Universum,* Pars I, tit. XV, *de consecratione episcoporum,* cap. 2, n. 24.

[27] Fagnanus, tit. XXIV, *de iureiurando,* nn. 73, 74.

or, if they enjoyed the rank of an archbishop, whether they convoked a provincial council every three years. Moreover, they were to indicate whether they had complied with the regulations of the Council of Trent regarding the visiting of their dioceses every year, or, in the absence of their ability to do this, at least every other year.[28]

The result of that diocesan visitation was to be made known to the Sacred Congregation of the Council. It was to be stated, for example, whether the faith had been preserved inviolate everywhere; whether any evil customs had arisen, or any superstitious rites or cults had arisen; whether pastors resided in their parishes, taught Catholic doctrine and otherwise fulfilled their parochial duties; whether the word of God was preached throughout the diocese at the accustomed times; whether any serious enmities or dissensions existed that could not be amicably settled; whether the practice of religion had decreased in any particular place, or whether the discipline of the clergy or the laity had become lax in any region or district.

In regard to the bishop himself, the report was to indicate whether he had been faithful in administering the sacrament of confirmation. The Sacred Congregation also wished to know whether a diocesan seminary had been built. It also sought knowledge whether the law of the cloister had been observed in convents and monasteries; whether the nuns followed the rule of the community life; whether any abuses had arisen in these holy places. Such were the questions that found a place in the questionnaire.

Bishops were obliged to indicate whether there was a daily distribution of alms at the cathedral church, and whether the canons of the cathedral were faithful in attending the divine services according to the prescriptions of the Council of Trent.

Finally, the report was to state whether the secular judges or magistrates had interfered, or whether any litigation had occurred with those authorities in affairs which

[28] Conc. Trident., sess. XXIV, *de ref.*, c. 3—Hardouin, X, 155; Mansi, XXXIII, 158.

pertained to the episcopal office, to ecclesiastical jurisdiction, or to the immunity and liberty of the Church.[29]

Section 5. Lawful Impediments Excusing from the Law

Because of the importance of the visit and report, Sixtus V wished to provide for any occasion and circumstance in which the bishop himself was unable to perform the duty. If he was detained by a just and legitimate impediment, he took an oath that all the necessary conditions would be fulfilled through a specific procurator.[30]

From the practice of the Roman Curia, one can learn that the Congregation of the Council approved the sending of a procurator by the bishop when the latter was impeded by any of these reasons: sickness or infirmity, advanced age, or finally a necessitated continuance of residence in the diocese for the discharge of imperative duties. Certain impediments could exempt a bishop even from sending a delegate to Rome, e.g., pestilence, hazards of travel (brigandage was notorious at the time), war and other difficulties which seriously impeded access to the Eternal City.[31]

If a bishop had been detained by some impediment, he was to seek the permission of the Congregation of the Council to perform the visitation through a procurator. He was to furnish due information regarding the aggravating circumstances. This petition he presented to the Holy Father, who personally passed judgment.[32]

The fact or existence of this impediment could not be acceptably established by means of an oath. Sixtus V clearly stated that some legitimate proof was required before a bishop could be released from this duty. A pre-

[29] Fagnanus, *ibid.*, nn. 77-79.

[30] Sixtus V, const. *Romanus Pontifex,* 20 dec. 1585, § 4—*Fontes,* n. 156.

[31] Catalanus, Pars I, tit. XIII, cap. IX, n. 15; Melchers, *De Canonica Dioecesium Visitatione cum Appendice De Visitatione Sacrorum Liminum* (Coloniae ad Rhenum, 1893), p. 125 (hereafter cited as Melchers).

[32] Benedictus XIV, *De Synodo Dioecesana,* Lib. XIII, cap. 6, n. 3.

scription in the Constitution demanded that the bishops bind themselves under oath to visit Rome personally at the called for intervals, unless they were legitimately impeded. A second oath in proof of the fact that an impediment existed was deemed vain and useless. If indeed a bishop had not reflected any qualms about perjury when he knowingly sent a legate without being lawfully detained, he certainly would not have felt any anxiety about perjuring himself by stating that the excuse was a valid one.

It must be concluded, therefore, that the existence of impediments had to be proved in other ways than by means of the oath of the one detained. Such a one, moreover, had to prove that he was unable to remove the impediment, for otherwise he was not excused.[33]

The agent who had been deputed to perform this duty had to possess certain qualifications also. He had to be specifically appointed for this obligation; he was to be a secular priest, preferably a member of the diocesan consultors or otherwise possessing some ecclesiastical dignity. If such a prelate was not available, then any diocesan priest could be chosen. If a bishop was without a clergy, the visitation could be made by any secular priest or member of a religious community deputed by the bishop. For the sake of convenience, the Congregation of the Council also permitted the bishops, when legitimately impeded, to delegate as their procurator one of their diocesan clergy living in Rome. In every instance the procurator had to have in his possession the special mandate from the bishop and the Congregation's permission which excused the ordinary. Furthermore, the procurator had to be well informed regarding the status of affairs in the diocese which he was representing, and he needed to be a priest of proven honor and zeal.[34]

[33] Fagnanus, tit. XXIV, *de iureiurando*, nn. 14-19.

[34] Sixtus V, const. *Romanus Pontifex*, 20 dec. 1585, § 4—*Fontes*, n. 156; Benedictus XIV, *De Synodo Dioecesana*, Lib. XIII, cap. 6, n. 3; Catalanus, Pars I, tit. XIII, cap. IX, n. 15; cf. also Pallottini, s.v. *Episcopus*, IX, nn. 44-55.

Section 6. Penalties

If bishops neglected to perform their duty regarding the visit and the report, either personally or, when impeded, through a procurator, during the time allotted them by the Constitution, they incurred the penalties set down in the Constitution. In order that the bishops would well understand the seriousness of this law, Sixtus V threatened the following *ipso facto* incurred suspensions for its nonobservance: suspension from entrance into their churches, from administering the temporal and spiritual affairs of the diocese, and, finally, from the reception of any of the revenues from their churches. These censures were to remain in force until the guilty party retracted his contumacy and sought a relaxation of the suspension from the Apostolic See.[35]

The law itself stated, and Fagnani made note of that fact, that prelates did not incur these penalties unless the very last day for the fulfillment of this obligation had passed and the performance of the duty had been neglected. Furthermore, if a bishop had been so negligent as to wait until the last moment before beginning to fulfill his duty and then the impediment arose, Fagnani held that he was still bound by the penalties as consequent upon his lack of proper diligence. In all these things, however, Fagnani pointed out that the Sacred Congregation was indeed most just and equitable.[36]

ARTICLE II. THE CONSTITUTION *Quod Sancta* (1740)

Three months after Benedict XIV (1740-1758) assumed the duties of the papacy, he gave official confirmation to the legislation which Sixtus X had established regarding the *ad limina* visit and report. This was a subject with which he had been closely associated when he served as Secretary of the Sacred Congregation of the Council. More-

[35] Sixtus V, *ibid.*, § 8; Lucidi, I, 31; Melchers, p. 126; S. C. C., *in Urbevetana*, 21 maii 1644—Pallottini, s.v. *Episcopus*, IX, n. 41.

[36] Fagnanus, tit. XXIV, *de iureiurando*, nn. 57, 58.

over, at the direction of Pope Benedict XIII (1724-1730) he had helped prepare an Instruction which outlined for the bishops the proper way for drawing up their reports to the Apostolic See.[37]

During his tenure of office in the Sacred Congregation of the Council Cardinal Lambertini, the future Benedict XIV, noted that one group of prelates had not received mention among those who were bound to the observance of the Sixtine Constitution. This document had not referred to those lesser prelates who governed their own territory as a truly separated district, in which they alone, independently of any bishop, exercised complete jurisdiction over the clergy and people. As a result, the law of Sixtus X had been interpreted as not applying to these lower prelates.[38]

It seemed incongruous that prelates of this kind, immediately subject to the Apostolic See, did not visit Rome and report on the condition of their administration as did others who presided over ecclesiastical territories.[39]

It was to remedy this situation that Benedict XIV extended the prescriptions of the Sixtine Constitution to include abbots and other prelates having quasi-episcopal jurisdiction for the government of truly separate territories.[40]

Benedict pointed out in his Constitution that the Pope was responsible to God for the spiritual welfare of *all* the faithful. Therefore, since he was bound to render an account of his stewardship to the Divine Master, the prelates of those monasteries and churches which were jurisdictionally independent of others were also to submit to him a report of their administration. At the same time he approved and renewed the previous legislation as it affected

[37] Benedictus XIV, *De Synodo Dioecesana,* Lib. XIII, cap. n. 10.

[38] Smith, *Elements of Ecclesiastical Law* (3 vols., Vol. I, 9. ed., New York, 1893), I, 343.

[39] Benedictus XIV, *De Synodo Dioecesana,* Lib. XIII, cap. n. 9.

[40] Benedictus XIV, const. *Quod Sancta,* 23 nov. 1740, § 4—*Fontes,* n. 303.

patriarchs, primates, archbishops and bishops, and he urged them to retain the vigor of their sacerdotal consciousness in observing this discipline.[41]

Before abbots, priors and other prelates with similar authority took possession of their monasteries and churches and began to administer them, they were bound by that Constitution to take an oath that they would visit the Holy See and present an accounting regarding their office. This duty was to be performed at designated intervals either personally or through a delegate. If they were in Rome and the Senior Cardinal Deacon was present, the oath was to be taken before him. In his absence, the legate of the Holy See could accept it, or any archbishop or bishop of the prelate's choice.[42]

As also in the Constitution of Sixtus V, the time for the performance of this duty was determined by the geographical location of the monasteries and churches. The abbots, priors and other presiding prelates (*praepositi*) of Italy and of the islands near Italy, namely, of Sicily, Sardinia and Corsica as well as of the provinces adjacent to Italy, were to journey to Rome and present their *relatio* every THREE years.

Prelates residing in the remaining provinces, kingdoms and regions throughout the world, where there were monasteries and churches with territorial independence then in existence or later to come into existence, were held to the provision of the law every FIVE years.

These periods began to be operative for all from the time of the promulgation of the Constitution, November 23, 1740. Newly elected prelates became bound to the obligation from the time they took possession of their jurisdiction.[43]

A special arrangement was provided for those abbots and others of like dignity who held office at the time the Constitution became law. If they had already been in pos-

[41] *Ibid.*, § 5. [42] *Ibid.*, § 6.

[43] *Ibid.*, § 8; Cappello, *De Visitatione*, I, 19.

session for two years or more, they were obliged to fulfill the prescribed duty within a year, if they lived within the boundaries of Italy or the adjacent islands; within two years, if they dwelt outside these limits. Thereafter the time of their visitation and report was to be determined according to the general computation mentioned above.[44]

If a prelate did not observe the precepts of this Constitution through his own negligence, he *ipso facto* incurred suspension a) from entrance into the church or monastery; b) from the administration of the spiritualities and temporalities of his territory, and finally c) from the acceptance of any revenue deriving from his monastery or church.[45]

ARTICLE III. THE DECREE *A REMOTISSIMA* (1909)

When the Sacred Consistorial Congregation issued the Decree *A remotissima* on December 31, 1909, it was the first major change in the Church's discipline regarding the *ad limina* visit and report in over a century and a half. During that interim, however, the Sovereign Pontiffs had never relaxed their vigilance for this law's observance, but through the Sacred Congregation had constantly urged bishops to a continued obedience to it. Pius IX on two occasions made particular reference to the importance of this episcopal duty, and gave special praise to the cardinals, archbishops and bishops of Austria, who had been so zealous and faithful in fulfilling the obligation.[46]

The Vatican Council (1870) confirmed and ratified the legislation of Sixtus V (1585-1590) and Benedict XIV (1740-1758) in regard to the law. The Fathers of the Council also directed that the Instruction of Benedict XIII (1724-1730), which contained the formula for the preparing of

[44] Benedictus XIV, const. *Quod Sancta,* 23, nov. 1740, § 9—*Fontes,* n. 303.

[45] *Ibid.,* § 10.

[46] Ep. encycl. *Optime noscitis,* 20 mart. 1854, n. 2—*Fontes,* n. 517; ep. encycl. *Singulari quidem,* 17 mart. 1856, n. 10—*Fontes,* n. 521.

the diocesan report, was to continue to be used by all the ordinaries.[47]

Moreover, the legislation of many plenary and provincial councils also served to remind the bishops of a particular country or province of the fidelity with which this law was to be observed.[48]

Here in our own country, the III Plenary Council of Baltimore (1884) incorporated the substance of an Instruction of the Sacred Congregation for the Propagation of the Faith relative to this obligation. This Instruction (May 3, 1875) was itself based on the Constitution of Sixtus V. According to the discipline of the Council, the bishops and vicars apostolic of the United States were to make the visit every ten years. The *relatio,* however, was to be submitted to the Sacred Congregation for the Propagation of the Faith every FIVE years.[49]

By virtue of the Constitution *Sapienti consilio,* issued on June 29, 1908, Pius X regulated anew the question of competence for the Congregation which was to examine the reports of the ordinaries. Thereafter, the reports of all residential bishops were to be submitted to the Sacred Consistorial Congregation instead of the Sacred Congrega-

[47] Martin, *Omnium Concilii Vaticani Documentorum Collectio* (2. ed., Paderbornae, 1873), tit. *de episcopis,* cap. IV, p. 131.

[48] Council of Mt. Lebanon (1736), Pars III, cap. 4, n. 9—*Acta et Decreta Sacrorum Conciliorum Recentiorum, Collectio Lacensis* (7 vols., Friburgi Brisgoviae, 1870-1892), II, 344 (hereafter cited as *Coll. Lac.*); Plenary Council of Thurles (1850), tit. XX, *de episcopis,* n. 7—*Coll. Lac.*, III, 791; Provincial Council of Cashel (1853), tit. II, *de episcopis*—*Coll. Lac.* III, 831; I Provincial of Westminister (1852), tit. XXIV, *de episcopis,* n. 3—*Coll. Lac.*, III, 946; I Provincial of Urbino (1859), Pars II, tit. II, *de episcopis,* n. 3—*Col. Lac.*, VI, 39; Provincil Council of Bordeaux (1868), cap. VIII, *de peregrinationibus ad limina Apostolorum*—*Coll. Lac.*, IV, 833; *Acta et Decreta Concilii Plenarii Latinae in Urbe Celebrati (1899)* (Romae: Typis Vaticanis, 1902), tit. III, cap. 1, *de episcopis,* n. 203.

[49] *Acta et Decreta Concilii Plenarii Baltimorensis Tertii (1884)* (Baltimorae: Typis Ioannis Murphy Sociorum, 1886), tit. II, *de episcopis,* nn. 13, 14.

tion of the Council.[50]

Prelates of missionary countries were not affected by this legislation, and therefore continued to submit their reports to the Sacred Congregation for the Propagation of the Faith.[51]

With the issuance, however, of this Constitution, the United States was no longer accorded the status of a missionary country, for it was withdrawn from the jurisdiction of the Congregation for the Propagation of the Faith and placed under the authority of the Sacred Consistorial Congregation.[52]

All this was as a prelude to the issuance of the Decree *A remotissima* by the Consistorial Congregation a year later.

Prior to the publication of the new law, the time for the visitation and the report had been arranged according to the geographical location of the dioceses, e.g., every three, four, five or ten years, dependent upon their distance from Rome. Moreover, the starting point of that computation had always remained December 20, 1585.[53]

The directions of the Decree *A remotissima,* however, determined that thereafter the time for the submission of the reports would be fixed and common for all the bishops of the Catholic world. Every bishop, therefore, regardless of the location of his see, was to present a diocesan report to the Apostolic See every five years.[54]

The time for the performance of the *ad limina* visit remained variable, but to a lesser degree than in the former law. As a result of the Decree, all bishops of Europe were

[50] Pius X, const. *Sapienti consilio,* 29 iun. 1908, I, 2°, 3—*Fontes,* n. 682; *AAS,* I (1909), 9-10.

[51] Pius X, *ibid.,* I, 2°, 3; I, 6°, 1, 3—*Fontes,* n. 682; *AAS,* I (1909), 9-10; 12.

[52] Pius X, *ibid.,* I, 6°, 2—*Fontes,* n. 682; *AAS,* I (1909), 12.

[53] Sixtus V, const. *Romanus Pontifex,* 20 dec. 1585, § 7—*Fontes,* n. 156.

[54] S. C. Consist., decr. *A remotissima,* 31 dec. 1909, can. II—*Fontes,* n. 2064.

to make the visit every FIVE years; the ones outside of Europe, every TEN years.[55]

The Decree stated that the *ad limina* visit could be performed either by the ordinary himself or by his coadjutor or auxiliary bishop. A priest could be delegated by a lawfully impeded bishop to fulfill this duty, but it was required that he be a permanent resident of the diocese of the bishop whom he represented. The Holy See had to grant approval before a bishop could delegate a priest to act as his procurator.[56]

The quinquennial periods were determined in such a manner that a fixed year applied in common to the bishops in the various particular countries, and were to be reckoned from the first day of January, 1911.[57]

If the year designated for submitting the report fell in whole or in part within the first two years after a bishop had taken office, he was excused from the obligation until the next assigned year.[58] The Decree excused those bishops who as a result of the old legislation would be obliged to make the visitation and report in 1910. Also exempted from the papal report and visit were those bishops who had performed the obligation in 1909 but who, according to the new law, would again be bound in 1911 or 1912.[59]

ARTICLE IV. FORMULAS OBSERVED IN THE PREPARING OF REPORTS

Section 1. Formula Issued by Benedict XIII in 1725

The *time* when bishops were bound to visit the Holy See had been determined by Sixtus V. Through his legislation it became obligatory for them also to submit a report of the status of their churches for consideration and examination. The provisions of that law did not indicate, how-

[55] *Ibid.*, can. IV, §§ 1, 2.
[56] *Ibid.*, can. IV, § 3.
[57] *Ibid.*, can. II, §§ 1-7.
[58] *Ibid.*, can. V.
[59] *Ibid.*, can. VI.

ever, any particular formula which the bishops were to follow in the preparing of their reports. It merely directed in a general way that they were bound to present an account *"de toto eorum pastorali officio, deque rebus omnibus, ad ipsarum, quibus praesunt ecclesiarum, statum et clerum pertinentibus."*[60]

The Holy See did not publish any formula, however, which the bishops might use as a guide in the preparing of their *relatio*. As a result the reports which were submitted to the Sacred Congregation of the Council frequently abounded in superfluities, or completely lacked the desired essential information.[61] Fagnani, as Secretary of the Sacred Congregation of the Council, had prepared an outline which the bishops could follow, but it never enjoyed an official status.[62]

To remedy that situation, Benedict XIII (1724-1730) at the Council of Rome in 1725 commissioned the Sacred Congregation of the Council to draw up an instruction which could prove of help to the bishops in the preparation of their reports. When the members of the Congregation had completed their assignment, the Holy Father approved the Instruction and gave it the authority of universal law.[63]

Although the Council of Rome was only a particular council, Benedict incorporated some of its decrees in the universal discipline of the Church, and the Instruction was given such a status.[64]

One of the principal assistants in the preparation of the Instruction was Cardinal Lambertini, later Benedict XIV,

[60] Sixtus V, const. *Romanus Pontifex*, 20 dec. 1585, § 4—*Fontes*, n. 156.

[61] Benedictus XIV, *De Synodo Dioecesana*, Lib. XIII, cap. 7, n. 1; Melchers, p. 131.

[62] *Commentarium in Secundum Librum Decretalium*, tit. XXIV, cap. IV, nn. 72-79.

[63] Council of Rome (1725), tit. XIII, cap. 1—*Coll. Lac.*, I, 364; Benedictus XIV, *De Synodo Diocesana*, Lib. XIII, cap. 6, n. 10; cap. 7, n. 1.

[64] Council of Rome (1725), Apendex—*Coll. Lac.*, I, 423-427; cf. Lucidi, I, 33; Ferreres, I, 656.

who at that time was serving as *Interpres Sacrorum Canonum* in the Congregation of the Council.[65]

The questionnaire comprised nine principal chapters or titles embracing the following topics: 1) the material status of the churches; 2) the ordinary himself; 3) the secular clergy; 4) religious orders of men; 5) nuns; 6) the seminary; 7) churches, confraternities and pious places; 8) the laity; 9) problems or difficulties which the ordinary could propose to the Sacred Congregation of the Council.[66]

Section 2. Formula Issued by the Consistorial Congregation in 1909

The formula prepared at the direction of Benedict XIII in 1725 remained in force until the promulgation of the Decree *A remotissima* in 1909. Appended to this latter document was a new questionnaire or schema, which the bishops were to follow in preparing their diocesan reports. This Instruction abrogated the use of the Benedictine formula.

The new arrangement was more comprehensive than the earlier formula, but the same general outline was followed in both. In the new schema, known as the *Ordo Servandus in Relatione de Statu Ecclesiarum,* sixteen chapters or topics were listed, and these were divided into one hundred and fifty questions. It was intended to furnish the Holy See with a complete survey of the general conditions of the diocese—economic, civil, religious and moral. The main topical divisions were the following: 1) general material status of the diocese; 2) faith and divine worship; 3) matters that pertained to the ordinary; 4) the diocesan curia; 5) the clergy; 6) the capitulars; 7) pastors and rectors; 8 a) the diocesan seminary, b) the regional seminary; 9) religious institutes of men; 10) religious institutes of women; 11) the laity; 12) schools and the education of

[65] Benedictus XIV, *De Synodo Diocesana,* Lib. XIII, cap. 7, n. 1,
[66] Council of Rome (1725), Apendix—*Coll. Lac.,* I, 423-427.

youth; 13) pious associations and societies; 14) pious legacies and the collection of alms; 15) social welfare and works of piety and religion; 16) printing and reading of books, periodicals and papers.[67]

When ordinaries prepared the report for the first time they were obliged to answer completely and accurately all the questions contained in the formula.[68] For the avoidance, however, of unnecessary repetition, subsequent reports had only to indicate that, with regard to the answers previously given to the questions contained in the individual articles, nothing new nor any change had occurred. When an increase or decline had taken place in statistical matters, the bishop was bound to note that fact in the next report. Furthermore, in the event that the Sacred Consistorial Congregation had given any instructions in response to a previous report, the bishop was to state what improvement or correction had been made in that regard.[69]

The report was to be written in Latin and signed not only by the ordinary but also by one of the diocesan co-visitators. This priest was bound to absolute secrecy; his divulging of any information which was not of a public nature was outlawed.[70]

Section 3. Formula Issued by the Consistorial Congregation in 1918

By virtue of the Constitution *Providentissima Mater Ecclesia* of Pope Benedict XV (1914-1922), a new code of canon law became effective for the universal Church on May 19, 1918.[71]

In order that the reports of the bishops might conform more closely to the prescriptions of the new legislation, the

[67] S. C. Consist., *Ordo Servandus in Relatione de Statu Ecclesiarum,* 31 dec. 1909—*Fontes,* 2065. Cf. *The Ecclesiastical Review, XLII* (1910), 703.

[68] S. C. Consist., decr. *A remotissima,* 31 dec. 1909, can. III, § 1—*Fontes,* n. 2064.

[69] *Ibid.,* can. III, § 2.

[70] *Loc. cit.*

[71] *AAS,* IX, Pars II (1917).

Consistorial Congregation published a Decree on November 4, 1918, containing a revised formula. The new questionnaire was to be followed by all ordinaries in the preparation of their reports after January 1, 1921, the first year of the third quinquennium. The formula which was found in the Decree *A remotissima* was thereby abrogated.

This formula will serve as the subject matter of the canonical commentary of this dissertation, and hence a more exhaustive examination of it will be made below.

Article V. Legislation for Ordinaries in Missionary Countries

Section 1. Residential Bishops

The Constitution of Pope Sixtus V had established that *all* bishops, archbishops, primates and patriarchs were bound to visit Rome and present an account of the condition of their dioceses at the times determined by the Holy See.[72] Pope Benedict XIV confirmed that law and extended it to include abbots and other prelates governing regions which were jurisdictionally independent of any other ecclesiastics.[73]

Now, in neither Constitution was any explicit mention made of those who resided in missionary territories. As a result of that omission, considerable doubt arose whether such bishops were bound by these Constitutions. Moreover, since these bishops had taken over the government of newly established dioceses, the Holy See was asked if the bishops of those dioceses that had been established *after* the publication of the law were bound to its prescriptions, and, if so, when was the obligation to be fulfilled.

In seeking a solution of that problem, one first of all must give consideration to the fact that neither Constitution made any exceptions in favor of the bishops who re-

[72] Sixtus V, const. *Romanus Pontifex*, 20 dec. 1585, § 3—*Fontes*, n. 156.

[73] Benedictus XIV, const. *Quod Sancta*, 23 nov. 1740, § 6—*Fontes*, n. 303.

sided in missionary countries; it was simply stated, without further reservations, that *all* bishops were bound. Moreover, the laws not only *did not* exclude them, but made implicit reference to such ordinaries when the time for the making of the visit and the report was established. Usually, such dioceses were the ones more distant from Rome, and accordingly the fulfillment of the obligation was called for every five or ten years. Likewise, the Sixtine Constitution made particular reference "to those regions which in the mercy of God would one day embrace the Faith."[74]

Furthermore, in the course of time the Instructions which were issued to the missionary bishops demonstrated that it was the mind of the Apostolic See that they were to fulfill this important episcopal duty.

In 1626, Pope Urban VIII (1623-1644), cognizant of the difficulties and circumstances peculiar to missionary countries, granted to their ordinaries the privileges of deputing a procurator living in Rome as their delegate for the making of the visit and report.[75]

In 1656, the Sacred Congregation for the Propagation of the Faith commanded that thereafter bishops and apostolic administrators subject to its directions were to submit a report of their diocese and to describe the boundaries, the condition of the Faith, and the number of Catholics.[76]

Again, in the year 1747, the same Congregation issued two letters on the subject of a report to the Holy See. One letter was addressed to bishops and vicars apostolic, and the other to prefects apostolic. The Sacred Congregation instructed these prelates to submit an annual report on

[74] Sixtus V, const. *Romanus Pontifex*, 20 dec. 1585, § 6—*Fontes*, 156.

[75] S. C. de Prop. Fide (C.G.) 28 iul. 1626—*Collectanea S. Congregationis de Propaganda Fide* (2 vols., Romae: Typographia Polyglotta S. C. de Propaganda Fide, 1907), n. 24 (hereafter cited as *Collectanea*); *Fontes*, n. 4432.

[76] S. C. de Prop. Fide, 3 febr. 1656—*Collectanea Constitutionum Decretorum, Indultorum ac Instructionum Sanctae Sedis ad Usum Operariorum Apostolicorum Societatis Missionum ad Exteros* (Parisiis: Typis Georges Chamerot, 1880), cap. VII, n. 88.

the state of their missions, giving the number of conversions, baptisms, etc.[77] Moreover, from time to time the Congregation found it necessary to remind the prelates of this important duty.[78]

Additional proof that bishops of missionary countries were bound to make the visit and report is obtained from the legislation issued by the Congregation for the Propagation of the Faith relative to vicars and prefects apostolic. If the Congregation imposed this obligation upon those prelates who governed areas that had not yet been established as dioceses, *a fortiori* all residential bishops had also to be considered bound by that law.[79]

In 1802 the Sacred Congregation for the Propagation of the Faith wrote to the bishops of Ireland, and in 1865 to a group of archbishops of the United States regarding the report and visit. The Congregation instructed these prelates that the triennial and quadriennial periods mentioned in the Sixtine Constitution were to be computed from the day of the Constitution's publication. Moreover, the recurring sequence of those periods was established *in perpetuum,* and without interruption it was to remain obligatory for *all* bishops.[80]

Furthermore, in order to assist bishops in the preparing of their reports, the Congregation from time to time issued special formulas which the bishops were to follow when they drew up the account of their administration.[81]

[77] S. C. de Prop. Fide, litt. encycl. 17 mart. 1747—*Collectanea,* nn. 362, 363.

[78] S. C. de Prop. Fide, 27 sept. 1843—*Collectanea,* n. 975; litt. encycl., 23 mart. 1844—*Collectanea,* n. 989; litt. encycl., 24 dec. 1849—*Collectanea,* n. 1039.

[79] S. C. de Prop. Fide, 28 iul. 1626—*Collectanea,* n. 24; litt. encycl., 31 oct. 1838—*Collectanea,* n. 877; (C.P., pro Sin.), 27 sept. 1843—*Collectanea,* n. 975; litt. encycl. (ad Vic. Ap Tunkin, Occident.), 23 mart. 1844—*Collectanea,* n. 989; litt. encycl., 24 dec. 1849—*Collectanea,* n. 1215; instr. (ad Vic. et Praef. Ap.), 1 iun. 1877—*Collectanea,* n. 1472.

[80] S. C. de Prop. Fide, instr., 1 iun. 1877, n. 6—*Collectanea,* n. 1472.

[81] S. C. de Prop. Fide, litt. encycl., 24 apr. 1861—*Collectanea,* n.

On May 3, 1875, the Congregation for the Propagation of the Faith decreed that all bishops were bound to make the papal visit and to submit a report, *even those who had recently assumed the government of new sees.*[82] The question was definitively settled in 1877, when Pius IX (1846-1878) approved an Instruction of the Congregation which declared that one of the chief duties incumbent upon *all* bishops was the making of the *ad limina* visit and the submitting of a written account of the status of their dioceses.[83]

Section 2. Vicars and Prefects Apostolic

In listing those who were to be obligated to the visit and report, the Constitution *Romanus Pontifex* did not include mention of vicars and prefects apostolic. Hence it was not certain whether they were bound to observe the law, even though they possessed episcopal or quasi-episcopal jurisdiction.

It must be noted, however, that as early as May 4, 1626, the "prefects" of mission territory were required to obtain an annual report from their missionaries describing the conversions, baptisms and other similar matters pertaining to the state of their missions.[84] Later the same obligation was imposed upon *vicars* and *prefects apostolic* and *bishops* who were then to forward that annual report to the Sacred Congregation for the Propagation of the Faith.[85]

In an encyclical letter of October 31, 1838, the Congregation for the Propagation of the Faith reminded arch-

1215; *Fontes*, n. 4853; instr. (ad Vic. et Praef. Ap.), 1 iun. 1877—*Collectanea*, n. 1473; *Fontes*, n. 4891.

[82] Cf. S. C. de Prop. Fide, instr. 1 iun. 1877, n. 8— *Collectanea*, n. 1472; The May 3, 1875 decree is itself not incorporated in the *Collectanea.*

[83] S. C. de Prop. Fide, litt. encycl., 1 iun. 1877—*Collectanea*, n. 1473.

[84] S. C. de Prop. Fide, 4 maii 1626—*Collectanea*, n. 22.

[85] S. C. de Prop. Fide, 20 sept. 1741—*Collectanea*, n. 331; 13 mart. 1743—*Collectanea*, n. 342; encycl., 17 mart. 1747—*Collectanea*, nn. 362, 363.

bishops, bishops, vicars and prefects apostolic and other superiors of missions of their serious obligation to submit the *annual* report.[86]

Answers given by the Congregation in 1844, 1849, and 1861 further clarified the responsibility of vicars and prefects apostolic. It was decreed that a) the prelates were to submit a complete and accurate report of their missions every five years; b) they were also to forward to the Holy See an annual report of the conversions, baptisms, etc., and c) they were, in addition, to observe the duty of the *ad limina* visit every ten years. The latter obligation could be performed by a procurator living in Rome.[87]

Because of doubts which still persisted in this matter, the Sacred Congregation issued a conclusive ruling on June 1, 1877. The Congregation declared that the Constitution of Sixtus V had been addressed only to ordinaries of canonically erected dioceses, and hence did not include vicars and prefects apostolic. Because of the office which these prelates held, however, the Congregation ruled that vicars were bound to the *ad limina* visit every tenth year, and that both *vicars and prefects* alike were obliged to submit a report of the status of their missions every fifth year. It was realized that there were difficulties and other circumstances involved in the long journey to Rome, and also that it was often not expedient that ordinaries be away from their territory for any prolonged period. Accordingly, permission was granted to vicars to satisfy their obligation through a procurator living in Rome. The time for the performance of that duty and also for the submitting of the report were still to be computed from the publication of the Sixtine Constitution, or December 20, 1585.[88]

Finally, in 1922, by mandate of Pope Pius XI (1922-

[86] *Collectanea*, n. 877.

[87] S. C. de Prop. Fide, litt. encycl. (ad Vic. Ap. Tunkin. Occident.), 23 mart. 1844—*Collectanea*, n. 989; litt. encycl., 24 dec. 1849—*Collectanea*, n. 1039; *Fontes*, n. 4829; litt. encycl., 24 apr. 1861—*Collectanea*, n. 1215; *Fontes*, n. 4853.

[88] S. C. de Prop. Fide, instr., 1 iun. 1877—*Collectanea*, n. 1472.

1939), the Sacred Congregation for the Propagation of the Faith published a new formulary which bishops, vicars and prefects apostolic and superiors of missions were to use in preparing these reports to the Holy See. The Holy Father declared that there was need of a revised questionnaire, which would be more in conformity with the regulations of the new Code of Canon Law that had become effective on May 19, 1918.[89]

Article VI. Formulas Observed by Ordinaries in Mission Countries

Section 1. Formula of 1861

It was the ruling of the Apostolic See that ordinaries of missionary countries were subject to the law of the Sixtine Constitution to the same extent as other ordinaries. These prelates, therefore, undoubtedly followed the same formulary in preparing their papal reports as did the other ordinaries throughout the world. There is no evidence of the issuing of a special schema for them by the Congregation until 1861. In that year the Congregation instructed all bishops, vicars and prefects apostolic subject to its jurisdiction that it was the wish of the Apostolic See that "in the future (the report) should be drawn up according to the formula of fifty-five questions, which was contained in the second part of the Instruction." The questionnaire was chiefly concerned with the character and knowledge of the priests working in the particular mission territory.[90]

Section 2. Formula of 1877

In an Instruction of 1877, the Congregation for the Propagation of the Faith declared that all vicars and prefects apostolic were bound to submit a quinquennial report, and that vicars were bound also to make the *ad limina* visit

[89] S. C. de Prop. Fide, litt. encycl., 16 apr. 1922—*AAS,* XIV (1922), 287.

[90] S. C. de Prop. Fide, litt. encycl., 24 apr. 1861—*Collectanea,* n. 1215; *Fontes,* n. 4853.

every ten years. The Congregation also published in this encyclical letter a new formula which the vicars and prefects were to use in preparing their reports. It was a more comprehensive questionnaire than the one issued in 1861. The new *ordo servandus* consisted of fifteen chapters comprising sixty-three questions, which pertained to the material and spiritual administration of the territory.[91]

Section 3. Formula of 1922

After the promulgation of the Code of Canon Law in 1918, the Sacred Congregation for the Propagation of the Faith prepared a formula which was to be in conformity with the new legislation. The Congregation instructed all bishops, vicars, and prefects apostolic and superiors of missions that the new formula supplanted the one issued in 1877, and that thereafter all reports (quinquennial) to the Holy See were to be made according to the new questionnaire.

This formula consisted of ninety questions, divided into seventeen chapters, which were entitled as followed: 1) general information concerning the mission; 2) the history of the erection of the mission and its division; 3) the ordinary and those who share in the government of the mission; 4) the clergy; 5) seminaries; 6) catechumens and the work of conversion; 7) pious institutions beneficial for the spread of the Faith; 8) education of the young in the lower grades; 9) education of youth in colleges; 10) the laity; 11) the administration of the sacraments; 12) matters pertaining to divine worship; 13) feasts, fast and abstinence; 14) churches, chapels and rectories; 15) cemeteries and Christian burial; 16) the administration of church goods; 17) a summary judgment of the material and moral condition of the mission.[92]

The report was to be written in Latin, and signed by

[91] S. C. de Prop. Fide, litt. encycl., 1 iun. 1877—*Collectanea,* n. 1473; *Fontes*, n. 4891.

[92] S. C. de Prop. Fide, litt. encycl., 16 apr. 1922—*AAS*, XIV (1922), 287-307.

the ordinary and by at least one of the canons or consultors, or one of the mission council[93] with a notation of the day, the month and the year in which it was prepared.

In the first report, *each* question was to be answered accurately and completely. That procedure was to be followed by every new superior of a mission the first time he submitted a quinquennial report.[94]

The Instruction stated that in subsequent reports the ordinaries were permitted to omit all questions which pertained to the historical and other general information of the mission territory.[95]

The Sacred Congregation for the Propagation of the Faith has not issued a new formulary since 1922. Hence, the ordinaries subject to its authority have continued to make use of this same schema in preparing their quinquennial reports.

[93] *Ibid.*, n. I.
[94] *Ibid.*, nn. II, III.
[95] *Ibid.*, n. IV.

PART TWO

CANONICAL COMMENTARY

CHAPTER III

PRELATES OBLIGED TO SUBMIT THE QUINQUENNIAL REPORT

ARTICLE I. PATRIARCHS, PRIMATES, ARCHBISHOPS, BISHOPS

The law of the Church has determined that *all bishops* are obliged to submit a written report every five years to the Sovereign Pontiff in regard to the state of their dioceses, according to the formula prepared by the Apostolic See.[1] In one sense, this is relatively new legislation, having its origin in the decree *A remotissima,* issued by the Consistorial Congregation on December 31, 1909.[2] By that decree the duty of the quinquennial report was *to some extent* separated from the *ad limina* visitation, and especially was this true in regard to the details the bishop was to follow in fulfilling that specific obligation.[3]

In prescribing the submission of a quinquennial report as one of the episcopal duties, the Code does not indicate whether every classification of bishops is obligated by the law. For that reason one could well advert to the various divisions of these prelates, and then examine their respective obligations, so that from this study the intent of the lawgiver might be better known.

Bishops are primarily classified as residential or titular. Residential bishops or episcopal ordinaries have both episcopal orders and actual jurisdiction over the clergy and laity of the diocese entrusted to their care. Titular bishops,

[1] Canon 340, § 1.

[2] S. C. Consist., decr. *A remotissima,* 31 dec. 1909—*Fontes,* n. 2064.

[3] Augustine, II, 364.

on the other hand, while they do possess episcopal orders, have no jurisdiction in virtue of their consecration even in their titular sees. There is assigned to these bishops a church or *titulus territorii,* in which the vast majority of the people are schismatics or infidels. In these areas the episcopal see has long since lapsed from its earlier active status. It was because of those conditions that these bishops were referred to as *Episcopi in partibus infidelium.* Even after these sees ceased to exist, the Sovereign Pontiff continued to name bishops for them, and it was customary for these prelates, who indeed possessed no jurisdiction, to be called *episcopi titulares.*[4] In 1882, the Sacred Congregation for the Propagation of the Faith decreed that that was the title by which this classification of bishops was to be known.[5]

Titular bishops are further classified as *coadjutors* and *auxiliaries.* Coadjutors or assistant bishops are titular bishops assigned by the Holy See to certain residential bishops for the purpose of supplying the insufficiency or inability of those bishops in the rule of their dioceses and in the exercise of episcopal orders.[6]

Finally, bishops may be classified as *suffragans* or *exempt.* The former are those who govern a diocese within the territorial limits of an ecclesiastical province over which a metropolitan presides. The exempt are those bishops or prelates who are immediately subject to the direction of the Roman Pontiff. Examples of this latter group would be retired residential bishops, apostolic delegates, papal nuncios and others whose office of assisting the Sovereign Pontiff in the apostolic ministry can be served more fittingly by one invested with the episcopal dignity.[7]

[4] Vermeerch-Creusen, Epitome, I, nn. 445 & 464; Coronata, I, n. 402; Wernz-Vidal, II, n. 572.

[5] S. C. de Prop. Fide, litt. encycl., 23 mart. 1882—*Collectanea,* n. 1565.

[6] Canons 350, §§ 1 and 2; 351, § 4; cf. Vermeersch-Creusen, *Epitome,* I, n. 464.

[7] Vermeersch-Creusen, *op. cit.,* I, n. 445; Coronata, I, n. 402; McElroy, *The Privileges of Bishops,* The Catholic University of Amer-

Inasmuch as suffragans are basically a division of residential bishops, and coadjutors, auxiliaries and exempt are, generally speaking, further delineations of the general category of titular bishops, principal consideration will be given to the obligation of 1) residential, and 2) titular bishops in reference to the quinquennial report.

A decree of the Sacred Consistorial Congregation under date of November 4, 1918, directed that a new and revised Formula had been prepared by the Holy See and was to be used thereafter by *all ordinaries* in drawing up their reports for the Sovereign Pontiff.[8] The new Formula was to replace the one issued by the same Congregation on December 31, 1909, and which was incorporated in the decree *A remotissima.*[9] In this latter decree it was stated: "... *omnes locorum Ordinarii,* quibus dioecesani regiminis onus incumbit, obligatione tenentur referendi singulis quinqenniis ad Summum Pontificem de statu sibi commissae dioecesis. . . ." The words, *ab universis Ordinariis* and *omnes locorum Ordinarii* of these two decrees indicate those prelates who are bound to submit a quinquennial report, namely, episcopal ordinaries or residential bishops who possess actual jurisdiction over a defined territory. The Code itself confirms such an interpretation. Canon 198, § 1, states that in law under the name *Ordinarius* are comprised the Roman Pontiff, and within their respective territories the *residential bishop,* the abbot and the prelate *nullius,* the vicar general of the foregoing, the apostolic administrator, the vicar apostolic and the prefect apostolic, as well as those who in the place of the above mentioned succeed to their right of government either by the provisions of law or in view of approved constitutions. These same prelates are comprehended under the term *Ordinarius loci.*[10]

ica Canon Law Studies, n. 282 (Washington, D.C.: The Catholic University of America Press, 1951), p. 5 (hereafter cited as McElroy).

[8] *AAS,* X (1918), 487.

[9] S.C. Consist., decr. *A remotissima,* 31 dec. 1909—*Fontes,* n. 2064.

[10] Canon 198, § 2.

Archbishops, Primates and Patriarchs are likewise bound to the provisions of Canon 340, § 1, not indeed by reason of their prelatial honor or title, but rather as residential bishops. Cappello[11] concurs with this distinction when commenting on the decree *A remotissima,* and declares that the words *omnes locorum Ordinarii* signify bishops, archbishops and patriarchs having their own proper dioceses to govern. Furthermore, this opinion is in accord with the teaching of the authors, and especially with the doctrine of the Holy See, ever since the promulgation of the Constitution *Romanus Pontifex* of Sixtus V. By this directive, it became formal law that all *bishops, archbishops, primates* and *patriarchs* constituted throughout the world, even those enjoying the cardinalitial honor, were obliged either personally or through the representation of others, to visit the reigning Pontiff and submit to him a report of their pastoral office.[12]

In 1740, Benedict XIV confirmed the legislation of Sixtus V when he decreed: "Easdem litteras Sixti V . . . confirmamus, ac etiam innovamus; omnibusque Patriarchis, Primatibus, Archiepiscopis, et Episcopis mandamus et praecipimus, ut eas sedulo ac diligenter et omnia in eis praescripta observare ac custodire studeant. . . .[13]

Moreover, though every bishop, before his episcopal consecration, was to take an oath that he would make the *ad limina* visit and render an account with reference to his full pastoral office, . . ."[14] as noted above, only a residential bishop exercised actual jurisdiction over a definite territory, and therefore it was only from that class of bishops that the Sovereign Pontiff expected and demanded a report.

Finally, this proposition is substantiated from the unanimous teaching of the authors. A search of the approved

[11] *De Visitatione,* I, 47.

[12] Sixtus V, const. *Romanus Pontifex,* 20 dec. 1585, § 3—*Fontes,* 156.

[13] Benedictus XIV, const. *Quod Sancta,* 23 nov. 1740, § 5—*Fontes,* n. 303.

[14] Catalanus, Pars I, tit. XIII, *de consecratione electi in episcopum,* cap. VIII; cf. Bouix, *De Episcopo,* II, 51.

writers reveals that there was no dispute about bishops, archbishops, primates and patriarchs being bound to submit a report to the Apostolic See.[15]

Following the promulgation of the Sixtine legislation, questions did arise, however, as to whether or not the Cardinal Bishops of the suburbicarian sees were also obliged to present a report to the Holy Father. It was the judgment of some authors that they enjoyed exemption from such laws because of their proximity to Rome, and in view also of the fact that as Cardinals they usually held important positions at the papal curia.

A precedent in this matter was perhaps established when Pope Urban VIII on November 28, 1633, rendered a decision involving the suburbicarian sees. This Pontiff declared that the Cardinal Bishops of those dioceses not only were *not* obliged to the law of residence, but, if they also held the administration of another episcopal church, they were to reside at the latter place. Cardinal Lorenzo Brancati (1612-1693) reasoned that they were exempt partly because of the nearness of their dioceses to the Eternal City. Being in such close proximity, the Cardinal Bishops could easily keep watch over the regimen of their jurisdictions and otherwise fulfill the duties of the law of residence—formally, if not materially.[16]

On January 9, 1616, the Sacred Congregation of the Council gave a decision declaring that the suburbicarian

[15] Wernz, *Ius Decretalium* (6 vols., Romae, 1898-1914; Vol. II, 1899), II, 913; Lucidi, I, 24; Cappello, *De Visitatione,* I, 47; Bouix, II, 51; Ferraris, Vol. V, s.v. *Limen Apostolorum,* n. 30, Ojetti, *Synopsis Rerum Moralium et Iuris Pontificii* (3. ed., 3 vols. and Index, Romae, 1909-1914), II, s.v. *Limen Apostolorum,* n. 2653 (hereafter cited as Ojetti); Raus (1881-1943), *Institutiones Canonicae* (2. ed., Parisiis: Emanuelis Vitte, 1931), p. 178 (hereafter cited as Raus); Cocchi, *Commentarium in Codicem Iuris Canonici* (8 vols. in 5, Vol. III, 4. ed., Taurini-Romae: Marietti, 1940), III, 189 (hereafter cited as Cocchi); Toso, *Ad Codicem Iuris Canonici Commentaria Minora* (5 vols. in 2, Taurini-Romae: Marietti, 1920-1927, Vol. II, 1922), II, 169 (hereafter cited as Toso).

[16] Cf. Benedictus XIV, *De Synodo Dioecesana,* Lib. XIII, cap. 6, n. 6.

bishops were not bound to the duty of the *ad limina* visit and report. The reigning Pontiff, Paul V (1605-1621), announced however that, though he did not wish to publish a declaration of this kind, at the same time he did not wish to impose the onus of that duty upon them if they were not bound. Nevertheless he intimated that it would be most pleasing to him if they also would comply with the general prescriptions of the Sixtine Constitution.[17] It can be noted, then, that at the beginning of the seventeenth century there was no formal, positive legislation obligating the Cardinal Bishops of the suburbicarian sees to submit a report on the status of their dioceses.

Pope Clement XII (1730-1740), however, proclaimed that these Cardinals were to be numbered among the prelates bound to the duty of making the report. He stated that "they should prepare a report of the status of their diocese over which they preside, and present it to the Supreme Pontiff according to the Constitution of Sixtus V."[18]

His successor on the Throne of Peter, Benedict XIV (1740-1758), gave complete approval to this decision. He wrote that the Constitution of Sixtus V made explicit mention of all bishops—even if they were Cardinals (*"licet Cardinalatus dignitate praefulgeant"*). Furthermore, since these Cardinal Bishops were obliged to visit their dioceses at proper intervals and to govern them according to the provisions of ecclesiastical discipline and were not exempt from any other episcopal duty except that of material residence, by what reason, he argued, could they be considered exempt from the law of the Sixtine Constitution?[19]

The present legislation of the Code does not explicitly state that suburbicarian bishops are bound to submit a quinquennial report. Canon 340, § 1, establishes this obligation implicitly, however, since it decrees that *all bishops* are subject to this duty. And when the law does not make any distinction, then certainly a distinction should not be

[17] *Ibid.*, n. 8.

[18] Const. *Pastorale Officium,* 10 ian. 1731, § 9—*Fontes*, n. 295.

[19] Benedictus XIV, *De Synodo Dioecesana,* Lib. XIII, cap. 6, n. 8.

invoked. Moreover, it has been noted above that, when using the phrase '*omnes episcopi*' the lawgiver had in mind those prelates who as residential bishops enjoy jurisdiction over a particular territory, and upon whom as residential bishops there was incumbent the duty of reporting to the Sovereign Pontiff on the exercise of that jurisdiction. Now, the Cardinal Bishops of the suburbicarian sees of Rome are residential bishops, and so they too become bound to the duty of the quinquennial report.

In addition, as was seen above, pre-Code law directed and commentators taught that the suburbicarian bishops were bound to submit a report to the Holy See. Since these Cardinal Bishops are at least implicitly mentioned in the provisions of canon 340, § 1—*omnes episcopi*—the provisions of the present legislation are in reality nothing more than a restatement of the earlier law and hence are subject to the same interpretation.[20] There can be no doubt, therefore, that the pre-Code discipline and jurisprudence directing that the Cardinal Bishops submit a report to the Holy See still is in force and is to be observed.[21]

ARTICLE II. TITULAR BISHOPS

It was stated above that bishops are primarily classified as residential and titular. A residential bishop has both episcopal orders and the power of jurisdiction over the clergy and the laity in a diocese that is entrusted to his care. A titular bishop, on the other hand, possesses episcopal orders but has no jurisdiction or authority even in his titular see.[22]

To be included within the general concept of titular bishops are "coadjutor bishops who subordinately assist a residential bishop either in the administration of his diocese or in the exercise of the duties arising from the episcopal rank or both."[23]

[20] Canon 6, § 2.

[21] Cf. Cappello, De Visitatione, I, 48.

[22] Wernz-Vidal, II, n. 572.

[23] Abbo-Hannan, *The Sacred Canons* (2 vols., St. Louis: B. Herder Book Co., 1952), I, 375 (hereafter cited as Abbo-Hannan).

The code distinguishes three kinds of coadjutor bishops: a) the coadjutor bishop given to the person of the residential bishop and constituted with right of succession; b) the coadjutor bishop given to the see; c) the coadjutor bishop given to the person of the residential bishop without the right of succession, and usually referred to as an auxiliary bishop.[24] The fundamental distinction between a *coadiutor datus personae episcopi* and a *coadiutor datus sedi* is that the former is appointed to assist the residential bishop in the exercise of both episcopal jurisdiction and the power of orders, while the latter seldom shares in the jurisdiction and administration of a diocese, inasmuch as the reason for his appointment is usually the necessity of the frequent exercise of the power of episcopal orders. Generally, the appointment of the *coadiutor datus sedi* is made because of the greatness of the diocese, so that he may aid the episcopal ordinary in the administration of the sacarments of confirmation, holy orders, etc.[25] But should it happen that the *coadiutor datus sedi* can properly fulfill the work of jurisdiction or administration in addition to his other duties, these should not be habitually delegated to anyone else.

All coadjutor and auxiliary bishops are, then, titular bishops who at the time of their episcopal appointment are named titular bishops of ancient episcopal sees whose territories have long since become peopled with infidels and schismatics and have ceased to be centers of Catholicity. Conversely, however, not all titular bishops are coadjutor or auxiliary bishops, for there are some who are consecrated for work in the Roman Curia or as papal legates.[26]

As can be expected, there exists among the three types of coadjutor bishops many divergencies but also some similarities regarding their rights and duties. But in reference,

[24] Canons 350, §§ 2 and 3.

[25] Chelodi, *Ius Canonicum de Personis* (3. ed., curavit Pius Ciprotti, Trento: Libreria Moderna Editrice, 1942), p. 304 (hereafter cited as Chelodi).

[26] Raus, n. 131; Coronata, I, n. 402.

however, to the quinquennial report, the canons give no indication whether this duty is incumbent upon each and every coadjutor. The Code does direct, however, that a coadjutor bishop should examine carefully the letters of appointment in order to determine what his duties are.[27] Other canons, though only in a general and indeterminate way, give further indications of the coadjutor's obligations and prerogatives.[28] But in order, however, that the purpose of this dissertation might be better served and repetition avoided in the discussing of the duties of each classification of coadjutor bishop, the writer has considered it best to divide the coadjutors into two classes: 1) *coadiutor datus sedi,* and *coadiutor datus personae habili* and 2) *coadiutor datus personae inhabili.*

Lynch, following the lead of Coronata,[29] observes this distinction between the two types of coadjutors given to the person of a residential bishop. He points out that the fundamental difference in their rights, powers and duties is not based on the question of their right of succession. Rather, it depends upon the mental and physical condition of the residential bishop whom they are appointed to assist —whether he is completely incapacitated (*inhabilis*) or is fully capable of directing the affairs of the diocese (*habilis*).[30] A further reason for following this division is the fact that the *coadiutor datus sedi* and the *coadiutor datus personae habili* hold identical authority as regards the source of their power of jurisdiction and administration which they possess in a diocese. Both are dependent on the will of the residential bishop in these matters unless their apostolic letters of appointment state otherwise.[31] The basis, therefore, upon which the distinction

[27] Canons 351, § 1; 352.

[28] Canons 351; 352; 354.

[29] *Institutiones,* I, n. 406.

[30] Lynch, *Coadjutors and Auxiliaries of Bishops,* The Catholic University of America Canon Law Studies, n. 238 (Washington, D.C.: The Catholic University of America Press, 1947), p. 58 (hereafter cited as Lynch).

[31] *Op. cit.,* p. 82.

will be founded is in their exercise of ordinary and active jurisdiction. Those coadjutors who do not possess it—*coadiutor datus sedi* and *coadiutor datus personae habili*—will be grouped under the general title of *titular*. Those coadjutors who do exercise such power—*coadiutor datus personae inhabili*—will be designated with the title *coadiutor.*

Section 1. Coadiutor datus sedi and coadiutor datus personae habili

Following the promulgation of the Constitution *Romanus Pontifex,* in 1585, the widest divergence of opinion regarding the ones bound to the law centered around the titular bishops. Andreucci (1684-1771) denied that these prelates were bound to the observance of the *relatio status dioecesis.* He reasoned that since such prelates were ignorant of the conditions of their churches, they were unable to give an accurate report of the conditions existing there. These bishops, he declared either reside in their own dioceses or they did not. If they did not, but remained in some Christian city without actual jurisdiction—as was the general custom—they could not reasonably be held to such a duty. In every obligation, he argued, attention was to be given to the very purpose inherent in the duty to be performed. The purpose of the *relatio* was to show due recognition and obedience to the Holy Father and to consult him regarding diocesan business and difficulties. He concluded that, since titular bishops were unable to discuss such diocesan affairs because of their absence from their sees, and since they did not hold any actual rule over the people, they could not be obligated to the law. He reasoned that their obedience to and recognition of the primacy of the Papacy could well be demonstrated in some other way determined by the Apostolic See.[32]

In 1662, after making a comprehensive study of this law,

[32] Andreucci, *Hierarchia Ecclesiastica* (2 vols., Romae, 1766), I, p. 76, n. 209.

Lucidi also held that titular bishops were not bound. He maintained this position, he wrote, because experience and extensive research of the papal archives had taught him that the reports of these prelates were not to be found among the documents preserved by the Sacred Congregation of the Council.[33]

A contrary opinion was offered by Fagnani (1588-1673). Titular bishops, he maintained, were bound since the captive condition of their churches did not prevent them from venerating the Tombs of the Apostles and presenting themselves to the Pope. In reference to their submission of a report, even though their churches were *in partibus infidelium,* he held that these prelates did not cease to be bishops of those places. It was Fagnani's contention that they were still bound to make enquiries regarding the status of their jurisdictions and be ready to offer to the Apostolic See such suggestions as might prove beneficial for the salvation of those forsaken souls and abandoned churches.[34]

In his commentary on the *Romanus Pontifex,* Thomassin (1619-1695) grouped titular bishops among the ones obligated to the *ad limina* visit and report. According to him, they were to explain to the Sacred Congregation of the Council the condition of the churches under their direction; what hope there was for the people returning to the fold; what attempts had been made to bring that about, and what progress had been made as a result of those endeavors. Thomassin referred to the treatise of Fagnani as the source of his opinion and, since he offered no objection to that position, it must be inferred that he was in agreement with it.[35]

Near the conclusion of his treatise, *De Synodo Dioecesana,* Benedict XIV stated: "In the visitation that bishops make to the Tombs of the Apostles, besides the veneration that must be shown to the remains of the Apostles, there

[33] Lucidi, I, 28; cf. S. C. C. *in Marochitana,* 1594; *in Poloniae,* 5 dec. 1637; *in Lubicanen.,* 27 febr. 1644—Pallottini, s.v. *Episcopi,* IX, nn. 36-39.

[34] Fagnanus, tit. XXIV, *de iureiurando,* nn. 82-85.

[35] Thomassinus, Pars II, Lib. 3, cap. 40, n. 13.

is manifest also a show of obedience and submission to the Roman Pontiff. Now, even a titular bishop, though absent and impeded from proceeding to his church, can know something of its status which should be reported to the Roman Pontiff. At the same time the titular bishop can also make proposals for the good of the church." And so he concluded: "Affirmandum videtur Episcopos quoque titulares ad Sixtinae Bullae observantiam teneri."[36]

In an earlier passage of the same work, however, Pope Benedict seemed to offer a contrary opinion, basing his conclusion on a certain decree of Clement VIII in 1594. The apparent disharmony is resolved when attention is given to the complete context of the first passage. There the opinion of Andreucci, on the one hand, and that of Fagnani and Thomassin, on the other, were being considered. The presentation of the latter two authors seemed more cogent in comparison with Andreucci's. It will be noted that Benedict followed closely and substantially the line of reasoning which was proposed by Fagnani and Thomassin, and since, in comparison with Andreucci's argument, it *seemed* more reasonable, he declared: *"Affirmandum videtur, etc."*[37] The contention that the above stated reference was not the belief of Pope Benedict but merely an appraisal of several authors' opinion is confirmed through the fact that in the earlier passage the Pope cited the Sacred Congregation of the Council and a decree of Pope Clement as authority for his stand that titular bishops were not bound to the obligation of the report.[38]

It was the common opinion of the later day authors that titular bishops were exempt from the obligation of the report. Their conclusion was based principally on the fact that such prelates did not possess ordinary and active jurisdiction over the territory to which they had been named. Wernz (1842-1914) wrote that titular bishops were not bound unless they were obligated to do so as a result of a

[36] Lib. XIII, cap. 6, n. 5.

[37] *Op. cit.*, Lib. II, cap. 7, n. 2.

[38] Bouix, II, 56.

special law, e.g., by reason of a particular office, or if they were Vicars Capitular.[39] Reference can also be made to a decision of Clement VIII in respect to the report as it affected coadjutors. The Holy See had been asked whether the duties of the *ad limina* visit and report were incumbent upon bishops to whom a coadjutor had been given. According to this decree of Clement VIII of February 25, 1592, as cited by Benedict XIV and Cardinal Melchers (1813-1895), it was sufficient if the ordinary himself or the coadjutor in the name of the ordinary satisfied this obligation.[40] It is to be noted that the decree refers only to the obligation of the *residential bishop*. The report *may* be made by the coadjutor, but this is done not in his own name but in the name of the ordinary. There is no mention of this duty as being incumbent upon the coadjutor as a coadjutor.

The law today does not list as an obligation of a titular bishop—*coadiutor datus sedi* or *coadiutor datus personae habili*—the duty of the quinquennial report.[41] The intent of the lawgiver to exempt these prelates from the observance of this law flows from the principles elucidated in the pre-Code legislation and discussed above. Summarily, it is due to their lack of ordinary and active jurisdiction. There is nothing which they might report to the Sovereign Pontiff regarding their titular sees. They cannot report the exercise of authority which they do not possess, and that is the basis of the law of the quinquennial report. Commentators on the Code are as one in maintaining that titular bishops are free of this responsibility. Unlike the divergence of opinions of the pre-Code authors, there is now no dispute on the question.[42]

[39] *Ius Decretalium,* II, n. 760; Bouix, II, 55; Ojetti, II, s.v. *Limen Apostolorum,* n. 2653; Melchers, p. 123.

[40] Benedictus XIV, *De Synodo Dioecesana,* Lib. XIII, cap. 6, n. 5; Melchers, p. 123.

[41] Cf. canons 351, 352, 354.

[42] Coronata, I, n. 402; Vermeersch-Creusen, *Epitome,* I, n. 460; Cappello, *De Visitatione,* I, 48; Cocchi, III, 178-179; Sipos, *Enchiridion Iuris Canonici* (Pećs: Typographia 'Haladas, R.T., 1926), p. 249

Section 2. Coadiutor datus perosane inhabili

The rights and duties of a coadjutor bishop are not determined on the basis of whether he has or has not the right of succession to the episcopal see. The determining and most important factor is, as canon 351, § 2, points out, the physical and mental condition of the residential bishop, i.e., whether the ordinary is *habilis* or *inhabilis.* As regards a *coadiutor datus personae habili,* the Code explicitly states that unless the apostolic letters decree otherwise, this prelate possesses only those rights and performs only such duties as are committed to him by the residential bishop. If the letters are silent in this matter, the Holy See should be apprised of the situation and the uncertainty will then be resolved. It does not seem pertinent to the purpose of this dissertation to discuss the connotation of the words '*habili*' and '*inhabili,*' or what is necessary in order that such a condition be predicated of the principal bishop. Suffice it to say that the apostolic letters of appointment will indicate whether the residential bishop is capable of ruling his diocese or not, and accordingly will define the rights and duties of the coadjutor bishop.[43]

On the other hand, the coadjutor appointed to assist a completely incapacitated residential bishop has all the rights and duties of the principal bishop.[44] Although he is not mentioned among those whom canon 198, § 1, refers to as an *Ordinarius,* he is properly entitled to that status by reason of the fact that he possesses complete and active jurisdiction in the diocese to which he has been assigned. As Wernz-Vidal declare,[45] the law reserves the title '*Ordinarius*' to those who exercise jurisdction in both the external and the internal forum. The office which the coadjutor

(hereafter cited as Sipos); Lynch, pp. 58-72, 80-82; Zitelli, *Apparatus seu Compendium Iuris Ecclesiastici* (2. ed., emendavit F. Solieri, Romae: Pustet, 1907), Pars I, *De Personis,* n. 325 (hereafter cited as Zitelli); Lucidi, I, 28.

[43] Cf. Lynch, p. 74.

[44] Canon 351, § 2.

[45] *Ius Canonicum,* II, n. 367.

fills as assistant to a totally disabled residential bishop satisfies this requirement, and, it is to be noted, for the entire diocese.[46] Since this coadjutor possesses the same rights and is bound to the performance of the same duties as a residential bishop,[47] it must be concluded that he too is required to submit a quinquennial report if the time for its presentation occurs during his tenure of office.[48]

Article III. Apostolic Administrators

Residential bishops, as a rule, administer canonically established dioceses. In the event the episcopal see becomes vacant, however, which may result upon the death, the resignation, the deprivation or the transfer of the incumbent bishop,[49] the diocese is provisionally ruled by the cathedral chapter or, here in the United States, by the diocesan consultors.[50] The Council of Trent decreed[51] and the present Code of Canon Law[52] has adopted the legislation that the cathedral chapter (body of diocesan consultors) is commanded to elect a vicar capitular (administrator) within eight days after obtaining knowledge of the vacancy. This vicar capitular (administrator) possesses the full administration of the vacant diocese until the Holy See rules otherwise.

There are extraordinary circumstances, however, when regardless of whether or not the bishop is in possession of his see the Sovereign Pontiff commits the government of a diocese to an apostolic administrator. The tenure of his office can be designated either for a certain period of time or, in rare instances, it can be a permanent arrangement.

The Code defines an apostolic adiminstrator as one to whom the Sovereign Pontiff, induced by grave and special

46 Lynch, p. 76.
47 Canon 351, § 2.
48 Cf. canon 340, § 1.
49 Canon 430.
50 Canon 431.
51 Sess. XXIV, *de ref.*, c.16—Hardouin, X,162; Mansi, XXXIII, 165.
52 Canon 432.

reasons, entrusts the government of a canonically established diocese, *sede plena* or *sede vacante.*[53]

These reasons or causes one can divide into two categories by following the general definition contained in the words of the canon. In the first division are the cases in which the diocese is not actually deprived of its bishop but in which the circumstances are such as to make him incapable of administering the affairs of the see properly. An apostolic administrator is customarily appointed to such a diocese (*sede plena*) when, as Vermeersch-Creusen point out, the bishop rules badly, when he is mentally ill, or when interference from the civil authorities prevents him from ruling properly. The second division pertains to cases occurring when the see is vacant (*sede vacante*). The Holy See will generally appoint an administrator to such a diocese when grave dissensions have arisen in the cathedral chapter (the body of diocesan consultors); when the vicar capitular (administrator) elected by the chapter (consultors) is unworthy; or when political discord warrants the appointment of a temporary administrator.[54]

Section 1. The Permanent Apostolic Administrator

The Code succinctly defines a permanent apostolic administrator as one who is sent by the Sovereign Pontiff to assume the government of a canonically established diocese which at the time is either occupied or vacant.[55] History has demonstrated that the appointment of such an administrator is far less frequent than that of a temporary administrator, and the reason is quite manifest. The presence of a proper bishop is more conducive to the regular and orderly direction of a diocese and is more in keeping with the practice of the Church. Furthermore, it is only

[53] Canon 312; cf. Cicogniani, pp. 113-114; Augustine, II, 326; Ayrhinac, *Constitution of the Church in the New Code of Canon Law* (New York: Longmans, Green & Co., 1928), p. 132 (hereafter cited as Ayrinhac); Woywod, *A Practical Commentary on the Code of Canon Law* (5. ed., 2 vols., New York: Joseph Wagner, 1939), I, 114 (hereafter cited as Woywod).

[54] Vermeersch-Creusen, *Epitome,* I, n. 331.

[55] Canon 312.

natural that the laity and the clergy of every diocese desire their own proper ordinary in preference to a permanent apostolic administrator.[56]

Occasions have arisen, however, when the appointment of such an administrator was necessary for the good of the Church. McDonough relates examples both in pre-Code and post-Code law when the Holy See joined a diocese by way of perpetual administration to another diocese in order to alleviate the financial burdens of the former, and hence eliminate the necessity of suppressing a diocese of ancient origin in the Church.[57]

There were other circumstances which could demand the the appointment of an administrator. There were, for example, instances when young nobles assumed the government of a diocese in temporal affairs.[58] An example of such an incident and its reference to the obligation of the quinquennial report can be found in the decisions of the Sacred Congregation of the Council in its interpretation of the Sixtine Constitution.[59] After the promulgation of this decree, there arose a situation wherein a young prince was appointed the spiritual head of a diocese. Inasmuch as he lacked the canonical age to assume the responsibility, an administrator had to be named to direct the affairs of the Church. When the Sacred Congregation was asked whether such an administrator was bound to submit a report to the Sovereign Pontiff on the status of the diocese under his direction, the reply was given that the administrator, first in his own name and then in the name of the Prince Bishop, whom he represented, was to observe the precept.[60]

[56] McDonough, *Apostolic Administrators*, The Catholic University of America Canon Law Studies, n. 139 (Washington, D.C.: The Catholic University of America Press, 1941), p. 159 (hereafter cited as McDonough).

[57] *Apostolic Administrators*, p. 162.

[58] Augustine, II, 326.

[59] Sixtus V, const. *Romanus Pontifex*, 20 dec. 1585—*Fontes*, n. 156.

[60] Cf. Benedictus IV, *De Synodo Dioecesana*, Lib. XIII, cap. 6, n. 5; Lucidi, I, 23; Melchers, p. 124.

The legislation favoring the permanent apostolic administrator with the same rights, honors and obligations as the residential bishop dates back to Decretal Law.[61] This decretal legislation granted the apostolic administrator, when he had been given complete administration of a diocese in both spiritual and temporal affairs, the same jurisdiction that was possessed by a resident bishop. There was only one reservation: if the administrator was not endowed with the episcopal character, he was obliged to call in a bishop to perform all acts of consecration. The same concept is clearly reiterated in the present law of the Code. Canon 315, § 1, states: "Administrator Apostolicus permanenter constitutus iisdem iuribus et honoribus fruitur, iisdemque obligationibus tenetur, ac Episcopus residentialis." The omission of any reference to the inability of the apostolic administrator to consecrate unless he is a bishop is understandable, since invariably the permanent apostolic administrator is a bishop. Both Toso[62] and Wernz-Vidal[63] point out that the permanent apostolic administrator is always a bishop, and very often the neighboring bishop or metropolitan.

It can be asserted, therefore, that the permanent apostolic administrator has always enjoyed the canonical status of a residential bishop in the legislation of the Church. The words of canon 315, § 1, grant him the same rights and bind him with the same obligations as the residential bishop. The canon makes no limitation of power nor is the scope of his duties restricted.[64] The permanent apostolic adiminstrator, like the residential bishop, is bound therefore to the precept of canon 340, § 1, i.e., to make a report to the Holy See about the status of his diocese.

Persecution has at various times ravaged the Church since the day when Christ constituted it. During the past thirty years, however, the scourge of Communistic oppres-

[61] C. 42, *de electione et electi potestate*, I, 6, in VI°.

[62] *Commentaria Minora*, II, 137.

[63] *Ius Canonicum*, II, n. 599.

[64] Cf. McDonough, p. 165.

sion has passed over many countries of the world with terrifying intensity. This has resulted in the denial of religious liberty to literally millions of Catholics, and in the confiscation of Church property. Further, it has brought about the death, captivity or imprisonment, the relegation or exile of many ecclesiastical rulers. For that reason, the question of what procedure is to be followed in the event the jurisdiction of the apostolic administrator would be impeded is a most practical one.

The question can be asked—when a diocese has become vacant[65] and the Holy See has appointed a permanent or temporary apostolic administrator[66] to govern it—who assumes the jurisdiction of the diocese if the authority of that apostolic administrator is impeded? The Code provides for such an emergency in the provisions of canon 317: "if the jurisdiction of the apostolic administrator is impeded or the apostolic administrator himself is incapacitated, notification of this fact must be sent at once to the Holy See; meanwhile, if the see is vacant or the bishop incumbent is not in possession of his mental faculties, the provisions of canons 429 ff. prevail. In all other cases, (*sede plena*) jurisdiction passes to the bishop (at least temporarily) unless the Holy See has decided otherwise for the particular case."[67]

Now, the jurisdiction of an apostolic administrator is impeded in the same way as that of a residential bishop,[68] i.e., by captivity or imprisonment, by relegation, by exile, or by some other personal disability.[69] In accordance with the direction of canon 429, § 1, the apostolic administrator is to delegate a vicar general or designate a priest who is to assume the government of the diocese, in that order, when the apostolic administrator has been impeded from doing so. In this regard, it is the opinion of McDonough

[65] By the death, resignation, transfer, or deprivation of a bishop's jurisdiction.—Canon 430, § 1.

[66] Canon 312.

[67] Cf. Abbo-Hannan, I, 344-345.

[68] Toso, II, 139-140; Cocchi, III, p. 164; Coronata, I, n. 383.

[69] Canon 429, § 1.

that the *permanent* administrator can appoint a vicar general, since he is in every way comparable to a resident bishop. The *temporary* administrator, however, since he is likened to a vicar capitular, is incompetent to appoint a vicar general unless the Apostolic See has explicitly given him the permission to do so.[70] The present legislation of the Church does empower a temporary apostolic administrator to designate a definite priest who is to govern the diocese when the jurisdiction of the administrator has become impeded.[71]

If circumstances should be such that: 1) the temporary apostolic administrator has neglected to delegate a certain priest to rule provisionally, or 2) the permanent apostolic administrator has not appointed a vicar general or named a priest to administer the see in his stead, or 3) after the apostolic administrator has been exiled, captured or relegated, the same fate should befall the vicar general and/or the delegated priest—the law of the Church declares that the cathedral chapter (diocesan body of consultors) should elect a vicar capitular (administrator) who will rule the diocese.[72] If the time for the submission of a quinquennial report occurs during his tenure of office, the rule for a vicar capitular in this regard should be followed. Because, however, of the temporary character of his position, he cannot be held to the fulfillment of this obligation. The administrator should seek the direction and advice of the Holy See in this matter. It could well be that the Sovereign Pontiff will wish to be fully informed in this instance because of the circumstances under which the Church would be existing, and for that reason the vicar would be asked to submit a report.

Thus far the consideration has adverted simply to the physical defects which would impede an apostolic administrator from properly administering a vacant see. Canon 429, §5, enumerates certain canonical impediments which

[70] *Apostolic Administrators*, pp. 219-227; pp. 152-158.
[71] Canon 429, § 1.
[72] Canon 429, § 3.

would hinder an administrator from discharging the functions of his office. When he is so impeded, it is the duty of the metropolitan or, in his absence, or if he is the bishop involved in the penalty, of the senior suffragan to have recourse to the Holy See in order that proper provisions for the government of the diocese may be made. The possibility of these circumstances occurring is, however, a slight one indeed. Yet the Church as a wise legislator has considered every eventuality. The improbability of their occurrence is based on the fact that the Sovereign Pontiff alone is competent to inflict punishment upon a bishop by way of a condemnation sentence or to certify its presence by means of a declaratory sentence.[73] Furthermore, should the Holy See deem it necessary to pronounce such a sentence, it is only reasonable to assume that, at the very time the sentence is given, provisions will be made for the proper administration of the diocese. Furthermore, the penalties specified in law as being automatically incurred may require a declaratory sentence for a necessitated ultimate observance.[74] The occasions would be most infrequent, therefore, when the administrator would be so prevented from exercising his jurisdiction.[75]

What is the duty of these substitute administrators in forwarding a quinquennial report to the Sovereign Pontiff? In every case presented above, the tenure of office of those who rule under such circumstances is indeed a temporary one. For that reason, it appears that they are not bound to the obligation. The Code does provide, however, that when such occasions do arise the Holy See is to be informed as soon as possible.[76] When that has been done, proper remedies will be invoked for a rectifying of the situation, and the substitute administrator will be made

[73] Canons 2227, § 1; 1557.

[74] Cf. canons 2264; 2232; 2227, § 2; 349, § 1, n. 1; 239, § 1, n. 2.

[75] McDonough, p. 180; Jaeger, *The Administration of Vacant and Quasi-Vacant Dioceses in the United States*, The Catholic University of America Canon Law Studies, n. 55 (Washington, D.C.: The Catholic University of America, 1929), p. 221.

[76] Canons, 317; 429, § 4; cf. *AAS*, VI (1914), 698.

cognizant of any further duties which the Holy See wishes him to fulfill.

Section 2. The Temporary Apostolic Administrator

It has been noted above that the temporary apostolic administrator is one assigned by the Sovereign Pontiff to govern, for a time, a canonically erected diocese. The existence of grave and special circumstances is the underlying cause for such an appointment. The diocese over which he is to preside may be occupied or it may be vacant. Oftentimes he is assigned to a diocese which he is to administer until prevalent abuses are corrected, or until a sick bishop is sufficiently recovered to reassume active administration, or until the return of a bishop who has been given a special assignment, *ad tempus,* outside the limits of his jurisdiction.[77] In such instances the temporary apostolic administrator does not possess the full and complete power of a resident bishop. On the contrary, the Code definitely states that the apostolic administrator who is temporarily assigned to direct a diocese is vested simply with the same rights and duties as the vicar capitular.[78]

In the succeeding article, the writer will discuss at length the question of the obligation of the vicar capitular to submit a report to the Holy See. He there concludes that the vicar capitular is not bound to do so. Because of his identity with the vicar capitular, the temporary apostolic administrator for the same reasons can be excused from any responsibility of making a quinquennial report.

Article IV. Diocesan Administrator (Vicar Capitular)

An episcopal see becomes vacant when the incumbent ceases to hold title or to be really its bishop. This may occur as a result of the bishop's death, of his resignation duly accepted by the Sovereign Pontiff, of his legitimate transfer, or of his deprivation of office pronounced in legal

[77] McDonough, p. 97.
[78] Canon 315, § 2.

form.[79] The death of the resident bishop constitutes the usual manner in which a see becomes vacant. Whatever the cause, however, when a see has become vacant, as long as the Holy See has not provided otherwise,[80] the government of the diocese devolves upon the cathedral chapter (body of diocesan consultors).[81] It is the duty, then, of that group to elect a vicar capitular (administrator) according to the provisions of the Code, [82] and this prelate will rule the diocese, with full power, in place of and as distinct from the chapter (board of consultors).[83]

The obligations which are incumbent upon the residential bishop, in general, apply equally as well to this diocesan administrator. This flows naturally from the fact that the administrator possesses the jurisdiction of the bishop and succeeds him as the ruler of the diocese and custodian of its spiritual and temporal affairs.[84] He can be truly called an *Ordinarius loci,* for he belongs to that classification of persons who, by the provision of law, succeed ordinaries in governing.[85] Although the administrator possesses the legislative, judicial, coercive and executive functions of the residential bishop,[86] there are several duties to the performance of which he is not held. In no place does the Code list as an obligation of the vicar capitular (diocesan administrator) the duty of reporting the status of the diocese which has been committed to his care. This omission is understandable when one considers the transitory character of the office of vicar capitular (diocesan administrator) and the very nature and purpose of the quinquennial report.[87]

The fundamental legislation upon which the present law

[79] Canons 430, 431.
[80] Canons 312-318.
[81] Canon 431.
[82] Canons 429-444.
[83] Coronata, I, n. 461.
[84] Canon 435, § 1.
[85] Canon 198, § 1.
[86] Canons 335, 336.
[87] Jaeger, p. 205.

of the quiquennial report is founded, namely the Constitution *Romanus Pontifex,* made no mention of this duty as regards those who presided over vacant episcopal sees. Lucidi made the observation that this omission was to be regarded as deliberate, since it would be a rare occasion when the Sovereign Pontiff would permit any vacancy to be prolonged beyond the time periods prescribed by the papal decree for the submitting of the report—three, four, five, and ten years! If it should happen, however, that the appointment of a new ordinary had been delayed for such a long time, there is nothing to prevent the vicar capitular (diocesan administrator) from making a report. He cannot be declared bound to do so, however, from the strict letter of the law. As Lucidi pointed out, it had been the customary practice that they did *not* perform this specifically episcopal duty. Usually a permission was requested from the Sacred Congregation of the Council to forego the submitting of the report until the Holy See had appointed a new ordinary. He in turn petitioned for and obtained an extension of time, so that he might better acquaint himself with the new diocese. He would then be better equipped for the presenting of a more accurate and satisfactory report.[88]

Such an intepretation is as equally applicable to the present legislation regarding the duty of the vicar capitular (diocesan administrator) as in the pre-Code law. It can be concluded, therefore, that for much the same reason as mentioned above, the text of the Code of Canon Law refrained from obligating the vicar capitular or administrator with the duty of submitting a quinquennial report. He indeed is not bound to do so.

Circumstances could occur, however, when the Holy See, out of deference to a sick and/or aged ordinary, would appoint the coadjutor of the diocese (*datus personae habilis* or *datus sedi*) as temporary apostolic administrator. Further, the tenure of his administration could embrace that period of time when the quinquennial report was to be presented

[88] Lucidi, I, 28; Melchers, p. 124.

to the Apostolic See. Now although the temporary apostolic administrator is not bound by the strict letter of the law to submit a report,[89] nonetheless, in the circumstances just described, it is advisable for him to apprise the Apostolic Delegation of the situation and await their directions. It is easily understood that the Holy See would be particularly desirous of being given a quinquennial report when such conditions have existed for any extended length of time.

Article V. Abbot "Nullius" and Prelate "Nullius"

Canon 323, § 1, states that an abbot *nullius* and a prelate *nullius* have the same ordinary power and the same obligations with the same sanctions as a residential bishop within his diocese.

This definition of the rights and duties of lesser prelates is relatively new. Prior to the advent of the Code, no general legislation was to be found which imposed the diocesan bishop's obligations upon them. There were particular instances, however, when the Holy See bound them to specific episcopal duties.[90] The duty of submitting the quinquennial report was an example.

When Sixtus V promulgated his Constitution[91] in which he obliged bishops to a periodic submitting of a report on the status of their dioceses, he did not make any mention that a similar duty was imposed on lesser prelates, such as abbots and prelates *nullius* who possessed quasi- episcopal jurisdiction over truly separate ecclesiastical territories. Benedict XIV corrected that omission by extending the provisions of the Sixtine Constitution to include these lesser prelates, so that they too became bound to inform the Holy See at regular intervals regarding the condition of their jurisdictions. Pope Benedict reasoned that, since these

[90] Cf. Benko, *The Abbot* NULLIUS, The Catholic University of America Canon Law Studies, n. 173 (Washington, D.C.: The Catholic University of America Press, 1943), p. 94 (hereafter cited as Benko).

[91] Sixtus V, const. *Romanus Pontifex,* 20 dec. 1585—*Fontes,* n. 156.

[89] Cf. canon 315, § 2.

prelates were superiors over jurisdictionally independent monasteries and churches, they too were to submit to him a report of their administration.[92]

The Code incorporated this law as one of the duties of the abbot *nullius*. Inasmuch as this superior exercises over his subjects the same jurisdiction as a bishop, there exists for him also a uniform participation in the episcopal obligations. Furthermore, the abbot or prelate *nullius*, like the bishop, is permanently the ordinary and immediate pastor of all his subjects, and hence he too is expected to submit a report to the Holy See on the exercise of that authority.[93]

Benedict XIV decreed that the *time* for the performance of this duty was to be determined by the geographical location of the monasteries and churches. The computation of that time as arranged by the Benedictine Constitution was less extensive than that determined by Sixtus V for bishops. Benedict XIV limited the computation to two categories. According to the Constitution *Quod Sancta,* abbots, priors and presiding prelates of Italy and of the islands near Italy, such as Sicily, Sardinia and Corsica, as well as of the provinces adjacent to Italy, were to present a report every *three* years. The same ecclesiastical superiors residing in the remaining provinces, kingdoms and regions throughout the world, were held to the provision of the law every *five* years.[94] Furthermore, the Pope ordered them *"ut visitationem praedictam, et insuper relationem, iuxta praescriptam alias Episcopis formam, omnino conficiant."*[95]

This same arrangement with reference to the time and the manner according to which the report was to be prepared remained in effect until it was abrogated by the new law which Pope St. Pius X introduced in 1909, and which was promulgated by the Sacred Consistorial Congrega-

[92] Benedictus XIV, const. *Quod Sancta,* 23 nov. 1740, §§ 4, 5—*Fontes,* n. 303.

[93] Canons 323, § 1; 334, § 1.

[94] Benedictus XIV, const. *Quod Sancta,* 24 nov. 1740, § 8—*Fontes,* n. 303.

[95] *Ibid.,* § 9.

tion.[96] As a result of this decree, the time for the submitting of the reports became fixed and common for all the *bishops* of the Catholic world. Thereafter every ordinary was to present his report every five years. This plan was adopted by the Code, and is the legislation followed at the present time.

Although this law did not explicitly mention abbots and prelates *nullius,* it contained an implicit reference to them. In recounting the history of the law of the report, as it affected bishops, the Decree looked to the Constitution *Quod Sancta* of Benedict XIV as a principal source. This was concerned primarily with abbots *nullius.* The Decree then added, without making any distinction between abbots or bishops, that *"omnes locorum Ordinarii, quibus dioecesani regiminis onus incumbit"* were subject to the obligation of the quinquennial report. The description *"locorum Ordinarii"* was predicable of abbots *nullius* so that they too were by the law bound to follow its directives as to time and the manner of submitting the report, just as the bishops were bound.

Now, the law of the Code is more explicit. It definitively states that the abbot and prelate *nullius* have the same obligations as the residential bishop.[97] One of the principal episcopal duties is the submission of a report to the Sovereign Pontiff every five years according to a questionnaire prepared by the Apostolic See.[98] The abbot and prelate *nullius,* therefore, are also bound to follow this regulation. They are to draw up a report by following the same formula and then must present it during the same periods as their diocesan counterparts, the bishops.

Article VI. Vicars and Prefects Apostolic

It is a provision of the Code that vicars and prefects apostolic are bound every five years to send an accurate

[96] S.C. Consist., decr. *A remotissima,* 31 dec. 1909, can. II—*Fontes,* n. 2064.

[97] Canon 323, § 1.

[98] Canon 340, § 1.

report to the Holy See in reference to all matters affecting their pastoral office.[99] This is an adaptation of pre-Code legislation.[100] Inasmuch as they are numbered among the *Ordinarii locorum* of canon 198, and since it is their duty as well as that of residential bishops to urge the observance of the laws of the Church,[101] the obligation of the report is a most reasonable one.

A letter of the Sacred Congregation for the Propagation of the Faith imposed this same duty on the superiors of missions not yet established as vicariates or prefectures apostolic.[102]

As canon 300, § 1, states, the general norm of canon 340 is equally applicable to vicars and prefects apostolic and to residential bishops. Therefore, if the year assigned for the making of the report falls within *any part* of the first two years from the time when the vicar or prefect took office, he can abstain from presenting a report for that time. A more detailed discussion of such a situation is given below.[103]

Similarly, the quinquennial periods are fixed and common for the vicars and prefects apostolic, as they are for the residential bishops. Those prelates, for example, who reside in America or on the islands adjacent to America should present a report in the years 1949, 1954, 1959, etc.; vicars and prefects apostolic of Africa, Asia, Australia and adjacent islands are bound to this obligation in 1950, 1955, 1960, etc.

Unlike the residential bishops, however, who forward their reports to the Sacred Consistorial Congregation, vicars and prefects apostolic and the superiors of missions are to submit their *relatio* to the Sacred Congregation for the Propagation of the Faith. The reports themselves which these two classes of ordinaries present, are substantially

[99] Canon 300, § 1.

[100] Cf. *supra*, pp. 91-93.

[101] Canon 336.

[102] Cf. S.C. de Prop. Fide, litt. encycl., 16 apr. 1922—*AAS*, XIV (1922), 287, n. III; Bouscaren, *Digest*, I, 192.

[103] *Infra*, pp. 121-126.

the same, though in detail somewhat different. The law would naturally demand more from a canonically established diocese than from a missionary territory, and accordingly has adapted the questions to the respective circumstances. A further difference lies in the manner in which the two groups of ordinaries prepare their reports. The report of the residential bishop requires his signature and his alone.[104] The quinquennial report of bishops, vicars and prefects apostolic and of the superiors of missions subject to the Propagation of the Faith must bear the signature not only of the ordinary but also of one of his consultors (canons).[105]

[104] *AAS*, X (1918), 487, n. I; Bouscaren, *Digest*, I, 202.

[105] S.C. de Prop. Fide, litt. encycl., 16 apr. 1922—*AAS*, XIV (1922), 287, n. I; Bouscaren, *Digest*, I, 192.

CHAPTER IV

TIME PRESCRIBED FOR THE SUBMITTING OF THE REPORT

Article I. Computation of the Quinquennial Periods

It has been noted in a previous chapter that the duty of the quinquennial report arose by way of customary usage in the early days of the Church. History discloses many instances when bishops reported matters of grave importance to the Sovereign Pontiff. Nevertheless, the making of regular reports was not part and parcel of the episcopal duties in the first centuries. The earliest vestige of this obligation is the practice of the suffragan bishops of Rome assembling in the Eternal City twice a year for the provincial councils. The early ecumenical councils had decreed that such gatherings were to be held in every province. During the sessions of these convocations the prelates were accustomed to give a report on the status of their dioceses.[1]

Using the biannual attendance at the Roman provincial councils as a starting point, a chronological record of the legislation which determined the periods when a diocesan report was to be made to the Pope might be divided in this manner:

A) 447—Pope Leo I (440-461) granted permission to the bishops of Sicily to send simply three of their number to the Roman Provincial Council, *held each year.*[2]

B) 590—Pope Gregory I (590-604) relaxed the discipline affecting the Sicilian bishops, so that they were

[1] Cf. Chelodi, p. 299; Sipos, p. 246; Cappello, *Summa Iuris*, I, n. 383.

[2] *Supra*, pp. 9, 10.

bound *once every five years* instead of *once every* three years.[3]

C) 743—The Council of Rome. The legislation of this Council required that *all* bishops consecrated by the Pope were obliged to take an oath that they would attend the Roman Provincial Councils. If their dioceses were near the territorial limits of the Roman Province, they were to be in attendance *every year.* If their dioceses were more remote, they were to come to the Eternal City at such intervals as were specified in the certificate which they signed at the time of their consecration.[4]

D) 1234—The Decretals of Pope Gregory IX (1227-1241). During the five centuries between the Council of Rome (743) and the compilation of the Decretals, it had become customary for all bishops to journey to Rome, to visit the Pope and to present some kind of report on their diocese. It was not obligatory, however, to do so. A new formula of an oath was placed in the Decretals and it was to be used by the prelates who were *confirmed,* who were *consecrated,* or who *had received the pallium* from the Pope. These were to make a yearly visitation to Rome. Because of distance or other circumstances, indults often allowed the making of the *ad limina* visit (which included a report) to be of less frequent occurrence. As a result, visitations were made *every year* by the *citramontani, every second year* by the *ultramontani,* and *every third* or *fifth year* by the *ultramarini.* English and Spanish prelates were permitted to make their visit *every third year,* and there were some ordinaries, *ultramarini,* who were sometimes allowed to make their appearance *every fourth year.*[5]

[3] *Supra,* pp. 10, 11. [4] *Supra,* p. 12. [5] *Supra,* pp. 28-39.

E) 1585—The Constitution *Romanus Pontifex* of Sixtus V (1585-1590). *All* bishops were to make the visitation and report *every three, four, five* or *ten years* according to the location of the country in which they possessed jurisdiction and the time was computed from December 20, 1585.[6]

F) 1740—The Constitution *Quod Sancta* of Benedict XIV (1740-1758. This legislation bound abbots and other prelates having quasi-episcopal jurisdiction to the making of the report. The duty was to be performed every *three* or *five* years depending on the geographical location of the monasteries and churches and the time was computed from November 23, 1740.[7]

G) 1909—The Decree *A remotissima* of the Sacred Consistorial Congregation. Every *residential bishop* was bound to present a diocesan report to the Sovereign Pontiff *every five* years.[8]

H) 1918—The Codification of Canon Law. The legislation of the Decree *A remotissima* was adopted almost verbatim. It remains in force to this day.[9]

Throughout this historical evolution there was noticeable the Popes' constant insistence on the periodic submission of a report. Yet, when the execptions to the general law are considered, one can observe the Apostolic See's wise consideration of varying circumstances, so that the obligation would not become an impossible burden.

The present law of the Code has been so formulated that the report is to be made with a proper measure of uniformity and regularity, but at the same time the law does not involve too great an inconvenience for the ordinaries throughout the world. The utility of such an arrangement is immediately evident, since it establishes a definite and unchangeable rule, thereby eliminating the possibility of countless doubts and controversies.

[6] *Supra*, pp. 43, 46-49.

[7] *Supra*, pp. 57-60.

[8] *Supra*, pp. 60-63.

[9] Canon 340, § 2.

The quinquennial periods, during which time a bishop is to submit his diocesan report, are now fixed and common.[10] Romani understands the term 'fixed' as meaning that these periods have been defined by the law and must be irrevocably computed from January 1, 1911.[11] The Code, moreover, refers to these periods as being "common," which signifies that they were established not for individual bishops but for all bishops of a certain region.[12] Thus the lawgiver has arranged the quinquennial periods in such a manner that a fixed year applies in common to all the bishops of particular countries and is to be reckoned from the first day of January, 1911. Accordingly, the arrangement of the intervals for the making of the report was designated in this manner: in the first year of the quinquennium (1911) diocesan reports were to be submitted by the bishops of Italy, of the islands of Corsica, Sardinia, Sicily, Malta, and of other small islands off the coast of Italy; in the second year (1912), by the bishops of Spain, Portugal, France, Belgium, Holland, Scotland, and Ireland with the adjacent islands; in the third year (1913), by the other bishops of Europe with the adjacent isles; in the fourth year (1914), by the bishops of all America and the adjacent islands; in the fifth year (1915), by the bishops of Africa, Asia, Australia and the islands in these parts of the world.[13]

This wise arrangement has removed many of the doubts and perplexities which were present in the old law. Each bishop has now been assigned a definite year during which he is to present his report. This is determined by the geographical location of his diocese. In truth, the present law considers primarily the country or the region in which the diocese has been established. Thus the law has been so

[10] *Ibid.*

[11] *Institutiones Iuris Canonici* (2 vols. in 3, Vol. I, 1941, Romae: Editrice "Iustita"), I, n. 487 (hereafter cited as Romani).

[12] Romani, *loc. cit.*, Regatillo, *Institutiones Iuris Canonici* (2 vols., Vol. I, 2. ed., Santander: Sal Terrae, 1946), I, n. 491 (hereafter cited as Regatillo).

[13] Canon 340, § 2.

formulated that in a particular country, e.g., in America, the ordinaries of those dioceses which are now in existence will make their reports in the same year as the bishops of those sees which may be established in the future. Consideration need no longer be given to the time of a bishop's consecration or the date of the establishment of a diocese.

This is in sharp contrast to some interpretations given to the law of Sixtus V. When the Holy See established a new diocese, it seemed that the triennium, quadriennium, etc., were to be computed *from the day on which the bishop first assumed administration.*[14] The consequence of such an interpretation could result only in great confusion and irregularity, since the bishops of the same nation would be making reports at many different intervals. There was no reasonable progression in the presentation of reports, and it could readily happen that a great number of ordinaries would arrive in the Holy See at the same time. Such a coincidence could defeat the very purpose of the *relatio.*

Moreover, when the Code established the quinquennial periods as being fixed and common to all bishops of specified groups of countries, it removed other doubts and difficulties prevalent in the old legislation. For example, the law of Sixtus V ordered that those prelates who were residential bishops at the time of the promulgation of the Constitution were subject to its provisions as of December 20, 1585.[15] On the other hand, for those prelates who assumed new positions of authority after the promulgation of the Constitution, the Law declared that the time periods became operative from the moment of their consecration, or of their reception of the pallium, or of their transfer to another diocese. The Sacred Congregation of the Council resolved many doubts when it interpretated this declaration to mean, *not* that the *time of computation of the triennium,* etc., was to be determined from the very day of consecration, etc., but rather that as soon as a prelate was

[14] Bouix, I, 55.

[15] Sixtus V, const. *Romanus Pontifex,* 20 dec. 1585, § 7—*Fontes,* n. 156.

consecrated, or had received the pallium, or had been transferred, there *began for him the obligation that entailed the making of a report.* Thenceforward such a prelate was to follow the general rule binding all bishops.[16] The orderly arrangement of the present legislation, expressed in clear and definite language, has closed the way to these uncertainties. Wernz-Vidal saw a special advantage in having these quinquennial periods fixed and common. It is contained in the fact that, when the Holy Father has received the reports of all the ordinaries of some particular nation within the limits of one year, he will gain a better perspective of the conditions in that nation.[17]

There is a further advantage in the Code's arrangement of the time periods. The reports are presented distinctly, separately and progressively. The Holy See will thereby avoid receiving an overly great number of reports in any particular year, and so will be able to examine them more easily, and, after a careful consideration, to give opportune counsel and direction.[18] It is a wise provision which the law has made, for the purpose of the legislation would be defeated if the Apostolic See did not have ample opportunity to examine well the reports which the bishops submitted. Benedict XIV was aware of this fact when he noted the multitude of business which confronted the members of the Sacred Congregation of the Council in examining the diocesan reports. For that reason, he deemed it necessary to establish a separate section in the Congregation whose particular function was the perusal of all the episcopal reports.[19]

The same situation prevailed during the pontificate of Pius IX. To correct it, he appointed additional officials

[16] Fagnanus, tit. XXIV, *de iureiurando,* nn. 37, 38; S.C. de Prop. Fide, instr. 1 iun. 1877, nn. 5-9—*Collectanea,* n. 1472; S.C.C. *in Montis Alti,* 1594—Pallottini, s.v. *Episcopus,* IX, n. 40.

[17] *Ius Canonicum,* II, *De Personis,* n. 607.

[18] Cf. Cappello, *De Visitatione,* I, 50.

[19] *Bullarium Romanum Pontificatus Benedicti XIV* (Prati: In Typographia Aldina, 1845), Vol. I, n. 8, § 2.

for this curial work. By this action he sought to avert the delays which had frequently occurred in the answering of the reports, and which had prompted many bishops to complain to the Sovereign Pontiff.[20] So serious was this condition that Bouix (1808-1870) thought it necessary to point out that a bishop was not released from the duty of preparing a subsequent report if he had not received a reply to the earlier one by the time the next one came due.[21]

The Code has divided the nations of the world into five groups, each being assigned a definite year within the quinquennium for the preparing of the report. 1911 was the year during which the bishops of the first group of countries were required to submit the *relatio*; an obligation which was then to recur at the end of each quinquennial term, or every five years thereafter. Here in the United States, the time designated for the American bishops was the fourth year of the first quinquennium, or 1914. The duty was then to recur in 1919, 1924, 1929, etc.

Is there any particular time during the year when the report is to be made? The Code does not define any precise day, week or month during the specified year for the presentation of the report. Nor has the *praxis curiae* of the Holy See ever indicated a preference as to a special time. The entire year is made available for the convenience of th prelate. He can submit the report at any time from January 1st to December 31st of the designated year. The span of an entire calendar year is designated as the duration or period of time in which the report can in accordance with the law be duly submitted.[22] The bishop, therefore, could rightfully submit his report on the very last day of December within the year that calls for the making of his report.[23]

[20] Bouix, I, 63.

[21] *Loc. cit.*

[22] Cf. canon 34, § 3, n. 1, with reference to canon 32, § 2.

[23] Cf. Fagnanus, tit. XXIV, *de iureiurando*, n. 43; Ferraris, Vol. V, s.v. *Limen Apostolorum*, n. 25.

Article II. Exception to the General Principle

The purpose which the legislator had in mind when establishing the duty of the quinquennial report was to provide the Sovereign Pontiff with exact information as to the religious and material condition of dioceses scattered throughout the world. It was realized, however, that a bishop could possess such knowledge only after a careful and thorough visitation throughout his diocese, upon an investigation of the annual parish reports, and in consequence of a study of the diocesan chancery books and statistics. But the gathering of such data requires much time. The formulators of the Code were also cognizant of the fact that frequently a bishop's appointment would be made at such times that he would not have sufficient opportunity to acquaint himself with the conditions prevalent in his new diocese before the date when the report would be due.

Canonical legislation wisely provided for such situations when it allowed the following exception: "If the year designated for the submitting of the report falls either entirely or in part within the first two years after the bishop has taken possession of a diocese, he can omit presenting a report for that time."[24] This is a generous concession to a newly appointed ordinary. It marks a definite departure from the old law. The triennium, quadriennium, etc., of the Sixtine Constitution were continuously in effect, even for recently assigned prelates, and they admitted of no such exceptions. According to the common interpretation of the Constitution *Romanus Pontifex,* in the event that a bishop died or was removed from office and had not fulfilled the prescriptions of this law, the successor became bound to do so within the period assigned for his predecessor. Thus, if a bishop had been consecrated on May 1, 1591, within the third year of the second triennium, and his predecessor had not conformed to the regulation of the Constitution for that term, then the new ordinary was bound to do so before December 20, 1591[25]

[25]Fagnanus, tit. XXIV, *de iureiurando,* n. 36; Lucidi, I, 37; Bouix, I, 54; Ferraris, Vol. V, s.v. *Limen Apostolorum,* n. 26.

[24] Canon 340, § 3.

It can easily be discerned how the fulfillment of such an obligation could become most difficult. Further, when the modes of travel utilized during those ages are recalled, the task will be understood to have been an almosot impossible one. It is true, however, that the Sacred Congregation of the Council was accustomed to grant an extention of time if the bishop considered the current period insufficient for the preparing of a satisfactory report.[26]

The present law, however, desirous of obtaining an accurate account of a diocese, allows the newly appointed bishop more time to acquaint himself with his see before holding him responsible for his first report. He is permitted to omit the report if the time for submitting it falls within the first two years after he has assumed possession of the diocese.

In making this concession, the canon does not say that the bishop *must abstain* from making the report if those conditions are present. He is given the choice of complying with the general norm of law or completely abstracting from it. This is evident from the very words of the Code, *potest abstinere*. Such reasoning in concordant with the purpose of the privilege. The Holy See is not concerned with a hasty, superficial, incomplete report. It is the intent of the legislation to furnish the Sovereign Pontiff with an accurate and reasonably complete account of diocesan conditions. A suitable amount of time, therefore, is alloted to the newly appointed ordinary to do that. If, on the other hand, this prelate believes that he can make ready a complete and satisfactory report before the expiration of the quinquennial period, he may do so.

Canon 340, § 3, also prescribes that this biennial period is to be computed from the time a bishop begins to hold office in his new see. Here in the United States, the years prescribed by law for the submission of the report are 1954, 1959, 1964, 1969, etc. Consequently, in accordance with the exception provided in the canon, an American bishop who has taken possession of his diocese *at any time*

[26] Fagnanus, *ibid.*, n. 48; Lucidi, *loc. cit.*

in 1952, 1957, 1962, 1967, etc., or at any time thereafter up to the year assigned, can exercise his prerogative of not submitting a report for the current period.

A case could be envisaged wherein a prelate, because of an emergency or some peculiar circumstance, takes possession of a diocese immediately upon receipt of the Apostolic Letters of appointment, but before his consecration. If an American bishop thus assumed the government of the new see in December, 1956, but postponed his consecration until February, 1957, the question could be asked: Would the American prelate be obligated to submit a report in 1959, or could he make use of the privilege accorded in canon 340, § 3?

The law of the report binds the bishop not *qua* bishop but *qua* ordinary. Now, a residential bishop acquires canonical possession of a diocese through the presentation of the Apostolic Letters, in person or by proxy, to the diocesan consultors (cathedral chapter). This action is to take place within the territorial limits of the diocese and in the presence of the secretary of the chapter or the chancellor of the curia, who is required to make a complete record of the proceedings.[27]

From the moment he is the ordinary of the diocese he assumes as one of his episcopal duties the one that looks to the making of the report. In the supposition as it is proposed, he became the ordinary of the diocese as soon as he took possession in December, 1956, and not only from the day of his episcopal consecration in February, 1957. He would be obligated, therefore, to submit a report in 1959. The bishop in this case could petition the Holy See for a prorogation so that he might have sufficient time to prepare the report. Moreover, the number of years which he must include in the preparing of the *relatio* extends from 1956 to 1959. It must be remembered that the Code does not bind the bishop to make a report for his predecessor. The Holy See is not so much concerned with having a mathematically accurate and photographically exact and

[27] Canon 334, §§ 1-3.

detailed picture of every diocese. The purpose of the report is to present a "moral" picture, so that the Sovereign Pontiff can see whether the Church is achieving progress or suffering a retrogression, and at what a rate, in a particular diocese. That is why the Holy See does not demand that every single year of the history of a diocese be included in one report or another. Cicumstances of death, transfer and the like militate against such rigorous demands. Moreover, if one period is not reported, a comparison with the previously submitted *relatio* can indicate to the Sacred Congregation what took place during the unreported period. For example: In 1944, ten schools were reported in a diocese. No *relatio* was submitted in 1949. Then the *relatio* of 1954 shows that the diocese possesses twenty schools, six having been built in the past five years. The Congregation knows then that four schools were constructed during the unreported period.

Another case may be proposed. An American bishop, for example, took possession of his see in 1952. By reason of canon 340, § 3, he did not present any report for the quinquennium ending in 1954. When he later makes a report in 1959, will he be obliged to span a period of five or of seven years in his report?

According to the norm of the law, the report is to be a *relatio "quinquennalis,"* and not *"septennalis."* The bishop would be required to make a report for only a five-year period, running from 1954 to 1959.

The following situation could also occur. An American bishop assumed the government of his diocese in 1947. He made use of the privilege accorded in canon 340, § 3, and correspondingly did not submit a report in 1949. He died in 1951, and his successor acquired canonical possession of the diocese in 1952. In 1954, this ordinary also makes use of the prerogative granted him in canon 340, § 3. In 1959, how many years must be included in the report? Would the ordinary be obliged to include the time that was passed over by his predecessor, or would he be bound to the five- or seven-year period during which he was ordinary?

Briefly, the second bishop (the one appointed in 1952) would have to make the report only for the last quinquennium (1954-1959). Moreover, a bishop is never bound to submit a report for his predecessor, or to include an account of the former's administration in his own report. Fagnanus and Lucidi made explicit mention of that fact in commenting on the old law.[28]

Finally, the bishop herein described is responsible only for the quinquennium running from 1954 to 1959, for the same reasons that were mentioned in the two previous cases.

The question may be asked: If one has been a coadjutor for a number of years, but succeeded to the see only in 1957 or 1958, may he omit the report? As was noted above, the law in regard to the making of the report pertains to a prelate *qua ordinary*, and not *qua bishop*. Moreover, the coadjutor who has become the ordinary could make use of canon 340, § 3, and omit the report which according to the general norm would fall due in 1959.

[28] Fagnanus, tit. XXIV, *de iureiurando*, n. 47; Lucidi, I, 36.

CHAPTER V

THE TEXT AND ITS PREPARATION

ARTICLE I. PREPARATION OF THE REPORT ("NORMAE OBSERVANDAE")

At the time of his consecration, every bishop takes an oath that he will submit a written report to the Holy Father at regular intervals on the status of his diocese.[1]

The obligation of making a "written" report is not as ancient as the obligation of the *ad limina* visit. Historical documents attest the fact that from the earliest days of the Church there was fully recognized first the custom and then the law in accordance with which individual bishops visited Rome and *presented a report* to the Apostolic See describing the condition of their dioceses.[2]

In his Constitution *Romanus Pontifex,* Sixtus V decreed, but only in a general way, that bishops were to submit a report *"de toto eorum pastorali officio, deque rebus omnibus ad ipsarum, quibus praesunt, ecclesiarum statum, ad cleri, et populi disciplinam, animarum denique, quae illorum fidei creditae sunt, salutem quovis modo pertinentibus."*[3]

In conjunction with this decree, the Holy See did not issue any official norm, however, which the bishops were to follow in preparing their *relatio.* As a result, some reports abounded in superfluities while others were lacking in necessary information.[4]

[1] *Pontificale Romanum Summorum Pontificum iussu editum a Benedicto XIV et Leone XIII Pont. Max. recognitum et castigatum* (2. ed., New York: F. Pustet, 1908), Pars I, p. 82.

[2] Cf. S. C. Consist., decr. *A remotissima,* 31 dec. 1909—*Fontes,* n. 2064.

[3] Sixtus V, const. *Romanus Pontifex* 20 dec. 1585, § 3—*Fontes,* n. 156.

[4] Benedictus XIV, *De Synodo Dioecesana,* Lib. XIII, cap. 7, n. 1.

Fagnani (1588-1678) drew up a questionnaire which served as a guide for the bishops in the preparing of their reports. This formula did not, however, enjoy the authority of law, even though it was an invaluable aid to the prelates.[5]

The obligation of making a *written report* and the manner in which it was to be drawn up were established by Pope Benedict XIII in an instruction of November 16, 1725.[6]

The Benedictine formula remained in force until it was abrogated by the Decree *A remotissima* in 1909.[7] Then on November 4, 1918, the Sacred Consistorial Congregation published a revised questionnaire, which was to conform more closely to the new Code of canon law, which had been recently promulgated.[8] This is the formula followed by all bishops at the present time who are subject to the Sacred Consistorial Congregation.

Besides answering the various questions contained in the formula, bishops are obliged to observe the following norms in drawing up the report.

I. "The report is to be in Latin, signed by the ordinary, and it must bear a notation of the day, month and the year."

In preparing their reports, ordinaries may well keep in mind the admonition of Pope Sixtus V, words of counsel that are applicable in every age. The venerable pontiff reminded the hierarchy of the world that the neglect of so salutary a law brought harm not only to their own souls but to their dioceses as well. It was to just such a disregard of ecclesiastical duties that Sixtus attributed, in part, the origin and spread of the Protestant errors.[9] The

[5] *Commentarium in Secundum Librum Decretalium,* tit. XXIV, cap. IV, nn. 72-79.

[6] *Supra,* pp. 83, 84.

[7] S.C. Consist., *Ordo Servandus in Relatione de Statu Ecclesiarum,* 31 dec. 1909—*Fontes,* n. 2065.

[8] *AAS,* X (1918), 487.

[9] Sixtus V, const. *Romanus Pontifex,* 20 dec. 1585, § 3—*Fontes,* n. 156.

ordinary, then, has a serious obligation to furnish the Holy See with a concise, clear, exact and sincere report on the condition of his diocese. Remote preparation for the fulfillment of this obligation is made by means of parish visitations and of a diligent examination of the annual parochial reports and of the records of the curia.[10]

The report may be written by hand, or a typewriter may be used. It is to be signed by the ordinary himself, and not by the vicar general or the coadjutor. Since the ordinary is the sole judge and authority responsible for the report regarding the status of the diocese, his signature is indeed required, but even alone it also suffices.[11] The bishop may assign a capable and discreet priest to assist him in the preparation of the report, but the final responsibiliy for its truthfulness and exactitude rests with the bishop.[12] Wernz-Vidal[13] remark that under the old law the co-visitators were also obliged to sign the report,[14] and hence were held to secrecy regarding its contents. For much the same reason, the chancellor or others who assist in drawing up the *relatio* are bound to secrecy concerning those things which have been learned from the report and are not public knowledge. It is Cappello's contention that they are bound to this secrecy not only in charity but also in justice. Divulging certain information contained in the report might bring harm to someone's good name or induce some other injury.[15]

II. "In the first report made by each ordinary, a full and exact answer must be given to every question in the formula."

In the first report, then, which the ordinary submits to the Holy See after having taken possession of the diocese,

[10] Regatillo, I, n. 491.

[11] Augustine, *Rights and Duties of Ordinaries* (St. Louis: B. Herder, 1924), p. 24.

[12] Romani, I, n. 487.

[13] *Ius Canonicum,* II, n. 607.

[14] Cf. S.C. Consist., decr. *A remotissima,* 31 dec. 1909, can III, § 2.

[15] *De Visitatione,* I, 52.

he is obliged to give a complete and accurate answer to each and every question contained in the formula.

Even in those instances wherein his predecessor has submitted a complete report for the immediately preceding term by answering every question in detail, the new ordinary is held to the prescriptions of this norm. Although this provision of the law may seem unnecessarily repetitious, it serves as an inventory which Rome wishes to preserve.[16] It is also an indication to the Holy See that the new ordinary has become fully acquainted with the conditions existing in his see. This is particularly exemplified by question one hundred in Section XII. There the ordinary is directed to set down, *especially in his first report* his appraisal of the material and moral condition of the diocese, what hope there is for future improvement, what major dangers threaten the well-being of the diocese.

III. "In subsequent reports the ordinaries may omit mention of all items relating to the material status of the diocese, as long as these items have not undergone any change since the previous report."

The formal status of a diocese includes the part of the *relatio* which has reference principally to the pastoral office and to all those matters which pertain to the government of the churches and which contribute to the welfare of souls.[17] Since the welfare of souls is the primary concern of Christ's Church, it will be to that section of the report that delineates the growth or the decline of Catholic life that the Holy See will give the closest attention.

The material status of the diocese is of secondary importance; furthermore, it may remain more or less static. When those circumstances are verified, i.e., when the material condition of the diocese has remained unchanged since the ordinary's previous report, he may omit, *if he wishes*, any mention of it. The rule is explicit in granting this choice to the ordinaries—*"omittere poterunt ea omnia."*

The questions of Chapter I are among those which partic-

[16] Augustine, *Rights and Duties of Ordinaries*, p. 24.
[17] *Supra*, p. 69.

ularly refer to the temporal status of a diocese. If no substantial change has taken place in the items to which the questions relate, then a mere reference to the eariler report suffices.[18] The important requirement upon which is conditioned the exercise of this prerogative is that all those matters which pertain to the material status of the diocese have remained the same—*immutata manserint*—since the previous report.

Finally, in preparing all succeeding reports, the ordinary shall add in what manner and with what success he has reduced to practice the directives and the mandates which the Sacred Congregation may have indicated to him in its reply to his previously made report. He shall also indicate what progress or retrogression has taken place in the diocese with reference to the faith and morals of the clergy and the people, or whether the situation has remained almost the same. The ordinary is also requested to express his opinions regarding the factors that have contributed to the bringing about of the extant conditions.[19]

Finally, in answering the questions contained in the formula, the ordinary should bear in mind that it is a *quinquennial* report and does not encompass a longer length of time than that. Questions 82 and 29b are good examples of where one might be misled into believing that the Sacred Congregation wishes an enumeration of conditions or statistics which would embrace a period longer than five years. However, the Congregation does not wish to know, e.g., the total number of clerics presently in the diocese who have been incardinated but only the number who have been incardinated in the past five years.

Article II. The Formula Proper

Section 1. General Notions Relating to the Material Status of Persons and Places

1. The ordinary shall indicate his name and surname,

[18] Cf. Augustine, *Rights and Duties of Ordinaries*, p. 25.

[19] Cf. Chapter XII of the *Formula Servanda in Relatione de Statu Ecclesiarum*—AAS, X (1918), 503.

his age, the place of his origin, the religious institute if he is a member of one, when he was consecrated, or, if he is an abbot, when he was blessed, when he assumed the rule of the diocese.

If he has an auxiliary bishop, the ordinary shall indicate whether he was assigned in subjective aid of the ordinary or in objective aid of the diocese.

2. He shall briefly outline the origin of the diocese, its title or hierachial rank, what special privileges it possesses.

   If it is a metropolitan see, he shall list the suffragan dioceses and the name of the ordinary of the appeal court in accordance with canon 1594, § 2.

   If it is a suffragan see, he shall indicate who is the metropolitan, and whether he attends the episcopal conferences convoked by that metropolitan or by another prelate.

   If he is not subject to any metropolitan, he shall show to which metropolitan he turns in the provincial council, at conferences and for the court of appeal, according to canons 285, 292, 1594, § 3.

3. Moreover, he shall indicate:

   a) the ordinary's place of residence along with the necessary indications for the addressing of mail;
   b) the size of the diocese, the civil government (i.e., state, nation), the climate, the native language;
   c) the total number of inhabitants living within the limits of the diocese, the principal towns; the number of inhabitants who are Catholics; if there are various rites, the number of Catholics belonging to each; if there are non-Catholics in these, groups, the number of each group and the sect to which the group belongs;
   d) what is the number of secular priests, clerics (from first tonsure on), and other students of the seminary;
   e) whether there is a cathedral chapter or rather a body of diocesan consultors; whether there are

any other chapters or any body of priests existing in the manner of chapters, or of a community group, and, if so, how many there are;

f) into how many rural vicariates, deaneries, archpresbyterates or other circumscribed territories the diocese is divided; how many parishes there are along with the number of parishioners in the largest and smallest; if there are any parishes that exclusively serve linguistic or national groups, were they established for particular families without reference to any territorial division, and, if so, by what right; how many churches or oratories there are in the diocese; and if there is any much-frequented shrine within the confines of the diocese, and, if so, of what character and status it is (Canons 216, 217);

g) if there are any institutes of men religious in the diocese, which they are, and what is the number of their houses and priest religious;

h) if there are any institutes of women religious in the diocese, which they are, and what is the number of their houses and of the professed members.

Section 2. The Administration of Temporal Goods, Inventories, Archives

4. In accordance with the civil laws of the particular locality, how is the right and capacity of possessing, acquiring and administering those things that are proper to the Church absolutely safeguarded; or, rather, is it restricted and, if so, what is the condition of the clergy and the churches?

5. Has there been established, under the authority of the Curia, a Council of Administration, and of whom does it consist; does the bishop consult it in administrative acts of major importance according to the prescriptions of canon 1520?

6. Do particular administrators, whether ecclesiastical or secular, of every church even the cathedral, or of

pious places canonically established, or also of confraternities, give an annual report to the ordinary on the conduct of their administration (Canon 1525)?

7. Are the provisions of canon 1523 observed concerning the manner of administration and the recording of receipts and expenses?

   Has canon 1526 been observed which forbids the instituting of litigations without the written permission of the ordinary?

   Has canon 1527 been observed which commands the refraining from all acts which exceed the ordinary administration?

   Has canons 1544 and the following been observed which refer to the quantatively serviceable endowment of pious foundations, their charters, and other similar matters?

8. Do those who have received trust funds for pious causes observe the provisions of canon 1516, especially regarding the report that must be submitted to the ordinary?

9. In the sale, mortgaging, exchange, short-term lease or long-term lease of goods, have the norms of canons 1530-1533, 1538-1542, been faithfully observed by all: and, if not, what remedies have been used?

   Indicate the principal transactions which have taken place concerning these matters.

10. In reference to the payment of tithes and of the first fruits of a person's income, are the laudable customs being observed through a safeguarding abstention from all harsh demands?

11. Are the prescriptions of canon 1182 regarding the offerings made for the benefit of a parish or a mission observed concerning their administration and the report that must be submitted to the ordinary; do the collectors refrain from annoying and troublesome demands?

12. As regards Mass stipends, how are the regulations

observed which canon 831 prescribes about the synodal tax?

How is the law of canon 835 observed which forbids priests to receive Masses which they cannot personally satisfy within a year?

How is the law of canon 841 observed which commands that all unsatisfied Mass stipends be transmitted to the ordinary?

How is the law of canons 843 and 844 observed which calls for the use of a special book for the entering of Mass intentions be kept by the individual priest and by the rectors of churches and other pious places?

13. Have inventories been made in duplicate of the immovable property, the movable property, and the sacred furnishings of every church, of the parishes, the chapters, the confraternities and other pious places which have been canonically established? Has one copy been retained in the particular place, the other sent to the Chancery Office, all according to canons 1296, 1522?

    Have proper precautions been taken, and in what manner, so that on the death of a rector of a church or of the superior of a pious work, the movable goods and church furnishings, are not destroyed or removed (Canons 1296, 1300-1302)?

14. Does the bishop have an archive erected and safeguarded according to canons 375-378; are the documents and books to which canons 470, § 3, 1010, 1047, 1107 refer kept there; from what year do the earliest documents date; are there any parchments and incunabula: have lists of these been drawn up and catalogued?

    Is there also a secret archive, or at least a safe which is immovable, in which the secret documents are preserved according to the rules of canons 379-380?

15. Does the cathedral church, all collegiate and parochial churches, the confraternities and canonically erected pious places have their own archives with documents

proper to each and with inventories of the movable and immovable property, and also with an index of all the documents?

Is a copy of that catalogue forwarded to the Chancery Office and retained in the diocesan archives according to canon 383?

Section 3. Faith and Divine Worship

16. Have any grave errors against faith arisen among the faithful of the diocese; does any superstitious practice or any usage foreign to established Catholic institution flourish in the diocese; has the disease of Modernism, Theosophism, Spiritism crept into the diocese and have any of the clergy been infected with these errors?

    What was or still is the cause of this evil

    Is there a Committee of Vigilance in the diocese; of how many persons does it consist and how successful has it been in achieving its purpose?

    Is the profession of faith together with the oath against Modernism demanded, and is it faithfully made by all who are bound to do so according to canon 1406 and the decree of the Holy Office under date of March 22, 1918?

17. Is divine worship freely exercised; if not, what are the sources of the hindrances; do they arise from the civil laws, from the hostility of perverse men, or from some other cause; what plan is being considered for the removal of these obstacles, and is it being used?

18. Are the rights of the Church regarding cemeteries fully and completely safeguarded, and can the canonical laws concerning them be observed, and are they observed (Canons 1205, ff.)?

19. In divine worship, in the veneration of the Saints, and of sacred images and relics, in the administration of the sacraments and in sacred functions, are the can-

onical and liturgical laws observed as regards rite, or also the liturgical language and chant?

In these matters, have any partcular customs crept in, and, if so, what are they; is care being taken so that they may be prudently removed, or rather, are they being tolerated, and, if so, for what reason (Canons 731, ff.; Canons 1255, ff.)?

Are there any pictures, statues or other objects in the churches which are not in accord with the sanctity of the place, or which are not in harmony with the liturgical laws? What is being done with a view to their removal? Are there barred from the house of God all civic gatherings as well as all public fairs even for pious causes (Canon 1178)?

20. Does the number of churches in the individual towns or parochial districts suffice for the needs of the faithful?

21. In general, are the churches kept tidy and clean, decently ornamented, and furnished with the appointments that suffice for their needs and purposes?

    Are there any churches that are poor, dirty, or in need of repair, and is anything being done to correct that situation?

    There shall be listed all such churches, if there be any, which are outstanding for their structural art, their paintings, and their costly furnishings and precious appointments. Is proper care being taken of these things?

22. Is entry into the church for sacred functions absolutely and always gratuitous (Canon 1181)?

23. Are the churches properly safeguarded against possible thefts and profanations?

    Are those churches in which the Blessed Sacrament is reserved, especially the parochial churches, open to the faithful for some hours every day according to canon 1266?

    How are canons 1267 and 1268 observed concerning the custody of the Most Blessed Sacrament in only one place and on one altar; and concerning the ornamentation and decoration of that altar; canon 1269, concerning the state and condition of the tabernacle; canon 1271, concerning the lamp in the presence of the Most Blessed Sacrament?

Section 4. Questions Pertaining to the Ordinary

24. The ordinary shall indicate what income he receives in his capacity of ordinary, whether it is derived from immovable goods, from public subsidy, from gifts to the Curia, from diocesan contributions, or from other sources; and are they sufficient?
    In what kind of episcopal residence does he dwell, and with whom does he live?
    Does he call for the payment of the cathedraticum, as it is specified in canon 1504, and in what measure?
    Has he, according to canons 1505 and 1506, imposed the payment of other diocesan taxes, and of what nature are these?
    Is he burdened by any debt as the ordinary of the diocese or as a private person; what measures has he taken to effect its cancellation?
25. Has the ordinary taken proper care of the episcopal household and of the property, movable and immovable, of the episcopal benefice by having an accurate inventory drawn up according to the provisions of canons 1483, 1299,§ 3, and 1301?
26. In the latest vacancy of the diocese, besides an administrator, was an econome also elected to care for the property of the episcopal benefice, and were matters handled according to canons 432, 433?
27. In what way does the ordinary fulfill the law of residence, with what frequency does he perform pontifical ceremonies, does he deliver sermons and by pastoral letters instruct the clergy and the people; what precautions does he take to have the ecclesiastical laws become known and be faithfully observed by all (Canon 336)?

28. With what frequency does the ordinary administer the sacrament of confirmation, and how does he provide if he personally is unable to respond to the needs on the part of all the faithful?

    Are the regulations concerning the age of the recipients of confirmation and regarding their sponsors observed in the conferral of this sacrament?

29. How many during the past five-year period have been promoted to sacred orders either by the bishop himself or by some one else? Has the bishop observed the laws about not promoting a) those who are not necessary or useful for the churches of the diocese according to canon 969, or b) those who have not completed at least the entire curriculum in the seminary (Canon 972, § 1)?

    Has the number of the ones ordained been sufficient for the needs of the diocese?

    Has the bishop incardinated any cleric, for what reason; and did he proceed in accordance with the laws of canons 111, ff.?

30. Have the rules of canons 877, ff. been observed in the granting of the faculty or the permission to hear confessions; and canons 893, ff. with reference to reserved cases?

31. In regard to sacred preaching, has the ordinary taken proper measures so that according to the Constitution of Pope Benedict XV and the norms issued by the Sacred Consistorial Congregation on June 28, 1917, all things proceed correctly; and especially that the provisions of canons 1340 ff. are observed in regard to the granting of permission to preach, and canon 1347 with reference to the manner and subject matter of preaching?

    Has the ordinary taken care that the desire as it is indicated in canon 1345 regarding the presentation of a brief homily on all feast days, is being observed?

32. Has the ordinary, and with what success, zealously

striven to deter the faithful by all means from marriages with non-Catholics, infidels, or unworthy persons (Canons 1060, 1064, 1065, 1071)?

33. Has the ordinary either personally or through someone else visited the entire diocese during the past quinquennium (Canons 343-346)?

    Has he canonically visited, besides places and things, books and archives, also the clerics themselves, speaking with and listening to them individually in order to learn how each one orders his life, with what frequency each receives the sacrament of penance, etc.? Has he also taken note of those matters which pertain to the fulfillment of legacies, and which relate to the stipend and the celebration of manual Masses; and was it manifest to him that all things proceed according to the law as it is stated in canons 824-844?

    And if he has detected any abuse in these matters, he shall draw up a report concerning them.

34. Has he celebrated a diocesan synod and in what manner; and when was the last synod convoked (Canons 356-362)?

35. If the ordinary is a metropolitan or the presiding prelate of episcopal conferences, has he convoked a Council or a Conference, and what was the date when it was held; who were present and what decisions were reached?

    If not, did he attend the provincial council or the conferences either personally or through a delegate (Canon 287)?

36. How does the ordinary fare with the local civil authority; has it always been possible to safeguard and maintain the episcopal dignity and jurisdiction so that the Church has never suffered any injury to its liberty and immunity, nor has disgrace come to the ecclesiastical state because of servility to human power, or in any other way?

Section 5. The Diocesan Curia

37. Does the diocesan Curia have its own building and is it sufficient and suited for its needs; if not, how can this defect be corrected?
    Give a list of the officials of the episcopal Curia, together with the names of the synodal judges, examiners, parish consultors, censors of books and other particular priests who aid the ordinary in the government of the diocese (Canons 363, ff.).
38. Describe briefly the qualities and the work of the vicar general and of the other principal assistants in the work of the Curia.
39. Is the income of the Curia derived from taxes, pecuniary fines and forfeitures, or from other sources? How is it expended?

Section 6. The Seminary

40. If the diocese does not have a seminary, what measures are taken to prepare priests for the priesthood? Is a sincere effort made to choose young men of good promise who are from the diocese in order to establish a native clergy; what success has attended this effort; where are they educated (Canon 1353)?
41. If the diocese has a seminary, list accurately:
    a) the number and position of those who are in charge of the schools' discipline, of those who are the spiritual directors of the students, of those who teach, and of those who are studying;
    b) the physical condition of the buildings and also of the summer villa;
    c) the income and the expenditure, that is, the active (assets) and passive (liabilities) status of the pious institute;
    d) the things that are recognized as necessary for improved condition of the Seminary.
42. Is there a division into a major and a minor seminary according to canon 1354, § 2?

And if prudence has directed or the condition of the diocese has demanded that only a minor Seminary or 'Apostolic School,' as it is called, should be established, indicate where students for the major Seminary are educated: is this accomplished in their own provincial, or regional, or inter-diocesan Seminary established by apostolic authority according to canon 1354, § 3? Give a brief report of its condition.

43. Have the following rules been observed:
canon 1356 concerning the seminary tax;
canon 1357 concerning the canonical visitation with reference to the seminarians and the proper observance of the rules;
canons 1358, 1360, 1361 concerning the discipline in the seminary, its economic condition, and the spiritual direction given there;
canon 1359 concerning the deputies responsible for the discipline and administration of the seminary;
canon 1363 concerning the students who should be admitted or excluded;
canon 1371 concerning those who should be dismissed or expelled;
canons 1364-1366 concerning the literary instruction and scientific training especially in philosophy and theology;
canon 1367 concerning the exercises of piety and devotion;
canon 1369 concerning the fostering of the ecclesiastical spirit and the imparting of the rules and canons of Christian urbanity?

44. Has the ordinary taken care that some notably pious and talented cleric be chosen to attend one of the Colleges, Universities or Faculties in Rome or elsewhere properly approved by the Holy See, that there he might pursue his studies (Canon 1380)?

Section 7. The Clergy in General

45. In general, does the clergy obtain what is needed for their livelihood on a respectable level?

Is there a home for the sick and the infirm priests, or is there provided at least some subsidy whereby they can be helped?

46. Is there a retreat house for the clergy, or also a house in which may be received such as are serving a term of penance?

47. With what success has the ordinary shown concern for clerics to fulfill the various duties recounted in:
canon 125 concerning sacramental confession and the exercises of piety;
canon 126 concerning the annual examinations for the junior clergy;
canons 131 and 448 concerning conferences for the clergy;
canon 133 regarding their living in the same home with women;
canon 134 regarding community life on the part of clerics, especially of assistants with their pastor (Canon 476, § 5);
canon 135 regarding the recitation of the divine office;
canon 136 with reference to the wearing of the ecclesiastical garb and tonsure;
canon 811 as regards the wearing of a cassock in the celebration of Mass;
canon 137 in reference to the regulation forbidding clerics to give bail;
canons 138-140, 142 regarding abstention for all things that are unbecoming to the ecclesiastical state, from worldly theaters and shows, and from the management of secular business?

48. To how many clerics has the ordinary granted the permission which is spoken of in canon 139, § 3, of working in banks, in savings associations, in cooperatives, in farm unions, or the like?
Did the ordinary grant this permission in consideration of the common good because the non-availability

of lay persons, or for the advancement of religion; do the same causes for its concession still exist?
Are the banks or savings institutions in which the clerics work conducted by reputable people and according to correct principles so that it is not a matter of impropriety for a priest to have part in the work there?
In these same institutions is the administration so conducted that there is no danger of bankruptcy in which the priest might become involved; and by what means has the ordinary made sure about the reliability of this knowledge that so such danger impends?
Finally, are there any priests who through being employed in these financial institutions have withdrawn from the religious practice of a priestly life and furnished occasion for some trouble to the ordinary?
If there are any, the ordinary shall describe the cases and propose suitable remedies.

49. Does the clergy show that obedience and reverence to their ordinary and the Apostolic See which canon 127 prescribes, and if there are any who fail in this regard, does the ordinary denounce them?
If there is present in the diocese a clergy of divergent rite and tongue, does priestly charity exist among the clerics, and what care does the Ordinary manifest towards them?

50. In general, does the clergy obediently accept the duties which the ordinary commits to them according to canon 128?
Are there any clerics who, although they possess great talents, prefer nevertheless to live in leisure and free from duties?
If there are any priests who attend lay universities, have they observed and do they observe the laws established by the Sacred Consistorial Congregation regarding attendance at such schools?
If there are any such priests, the ordinary shall list them.

51. Are there any priests who write for the daily newspapers or periodicals or edit them; with what authorization do they perform this task and with what measure of usefulness or advantage (Canon 1386, § 1)?

52. Are there present among the clergy any who give scandal by reading the dailies and periodicals or books which are unbecoming to the clerical state?

    Are there any who unduly become involved in municipal factions or politics?

    Are there any who have been reduced to the lay state or because of some crime have of their own accord returned to that state (Canons 211-214)?

    What has been done to remedy these evils?

53. Has the ordinary inflicted any of the penalties delineated in canon 2298 and with what success? If he has, he shall list the more serious cases.

Section 8. Cathedral Chapters

54. If there is no cathedral chapter, then the ordinary shall list the number of diocesan consultors and indicate whether in their regard there have been observed all the directions which canons 424-428 prescribe.

55. If there is a cathedral chapter, he shall indicate of how many dignitaries and canons it consists.

    Are there a canon theologian and a canon penitentiary, and are the rules of canons 398-401 obeyed by them? Are there other lesser beneficiaries, and how many?

56. What is the endowment of the chapter or of its beneficed members?

    Are there applicable and are there observed the rules of canon 395 regarding the discipline of the distribution of the gratuities and the noting of absentees from the divine office?

57. If there are canonries of benefices that are subject to patronage, has the ordinary taken proper measures, and with what success, that the patrons accept spiritual benefits, according to canon 1451 in lieu of the

right of patronage which they possess, or at least in place of their right of presentation?

58. Does each chapter have its own statutes according to canons 410 and 416?
59. How many honorary canons are there in the diocese, and are the rules of canon 406 observed concerning them?
60. During the vacancy of the see, what plan is followed in the making of provision for the proper government of the diocese?
    When the see was last vacant, was the discipline of canons 429-443 observed?
61. Furnish some indication of the manner in which the chapter performs the sacred functions, of the way in which it conducts itself in its relationship with the ordinary, and also of other matters which pertain to its good name.
62. If there are chapters in the diocese, especially such as enjoy preferntial rank, or if there are clerical community groups which are established after the manner of chapters, the ordinary shall, with reference to them, submit a report analogous to the one that is required for the cathedral chapter.

Section 9. Vicars Forane and Pastors

63. Indicate whether the rural deans diligently fulfill all those duties which canon 447 prescribes regarding due watchfulness over the ecclesiastics of their district; regarding the care they should have that the canonical laws and decrees of the ordinary are observed and regarding other matters.
    Do they visit the parishes of their district according to the directions of the ordinary?
    Do they give an annual report to the ordinary on the state of their district (vicariatus) according to canon 449?
64. Are all the parishes provided with their own pastor; is the law of canon 460 observed, in reference to hav-

ing only one pastor in each parish, every contrary custom being rejected and every contravening privilege revoked?

65. Are there any parishes whose incumbents are removable pastors, how many of these are there, and for what reason were they established?
How many parishes are united to chapters, either cathedral or collegiate, to a religious house or to any other moral person?
In such cases, are the laws observed about the appointing of a vicar with a free exercise of the care of souls according to the prescriptions of canons 415, 471, 609, § 1?
And if a religious is a pastor, are the provisions contained in canons 630, 631 fully and completely safeguarded?

66. Are there any parishes, and, if so, how many, that are subject to the right of patronage? With what success has the local ordinary taken steps to have patrons accept in lieu of the rights of patronage, or at least in place of their right of presentation, spiritual benefits according to canon 1451? If the ordinary has been unable to do so, then, when the right of presentation exists, are there observed the laws as they are enacted in canons 1457, ff., and especially in canon 1452, when the people themselves have the right of election or of presentation?

67. Are the parochial appointments which are undertaken as acts of full conferment based on a competitive examination and by what method is the examination concluded (Canons 455, ff.)?

68. What is the source of the pastor's income? Does it derive from real estate (*ex immobilibus*), from a public fund or the public treasury, from an uncertified sum accruing through individual stole fees, or from a contribution made by the faithful or by the diocese?
In general, do the pastors enjoy a frugal but comfort-

able livelihood, and are there any who suffer from real want?

Have the pastors been provided with their own parochial house, at least one that has been rented and is sufficient for their needs?

If not, are there plans for or is there any probability of due provisions in this regard?

69. Do the pastors, in general, satisfy those laws which the following canons prescribe:

canon 463, § 4, concerning the gratuitious service to those who are unable to pay;

canon 465 concerning residence;

canon 466 concerning the application of Mass for the people;

canon 467 concerning the administration of the sacraments and zeal for souls;

canon 468 about care for the sick;

canon 469 as regards vigilance lest errors against faith and other evils arise; about instituting and fostering works of charity, faith and piety in his parish;
canon 470 which concerns the accurate keeping of the parochial records; and about sending an authentic copy of these registers to the Chancery every year;
canon 735 about the sacred oils being kept in a safe and decent place.

70. Concerning baptism: does every parochial church have a baptismal font according to canon 774? Whenever infants cannot be brought to the parochial church without danger or serious inconvenience, does the pastor spontaneously and willingly go to the nearest church or public oratory to administer the sacrament in accordance with canon 775?

71. Concerning the Most Holy Eucharist: Are the pastors filled with an untiring zeal so that, according to canon 863, the faithful are often, even daily, refreshed with the Eucharistic bread;

So that, according to canon 865, the sick receive Holy

Viaticum while they are in the full possession of their senses;

So that, according to canons 1273, 1274, and 1275, devotion to the Most Blessed Sacrament is increased through the encouragement of the faithful to assist daily at Mass and to make nightly visits to the Blessed Sacrament, and through the exposition of the Blessed Sacrament at stated times and conducting and promoting of other fruitful practices;

So that according to canon 854, with a due safeguarding of the right of the parents and confessors to judge whether children are properly disposed to receive first Holy Communion, those same parents will not neglect their duty and other abuses will not creep in?

72. Concerning Extreme Unction: are the pastors vigilant so that this sacrament is received by the sick while they are still in full possession of their senses?

73. Concerning the celebration of marriage: are all pastors diligent in observing the prescriptions contained in the Code of Canon Law, Book III, Title VII, which concern the free state of the contracting parties, dispensation from the impediments, the use of sacred rites, and the inscribing of the celebration of the marriage in the proper register?

74. Concerning catechetical instruction: do all pastors diligently observe all those laws which are established in:

canon 1330 about a special series of catechetical instructions in preparation for the first confession, first Holy Communion, and the confirmation of children;

canons 1331-1336 on the imparting of catechetical instructions on feast days to children and adults alike?

75. Concerning the explanation of the Holy Gospel: Is the law of canon 1344 observed by all;

Concerning preaching: are sacred sermons preached with added frequency at certain stated times, as the law of canon 1346 requires, and are missions held according to the prescriptions of canon 1349?

76. Do assistant pastors and others having the care of souls discharge their duties in a praiseworthy manner according to canons 473, ff.?

Section 10. Religious

77. Has the ordinary either personally or through a delegate made the quinquennial visitation of the religious houses according to canons 512, 513; and what are the more important items for report?

78. Do the religious, both men and women, follow the common life; are there any who dwell alone or in private homes with the laity, and by what right?

    In either case, what is their reputation;

    How is this advantageous for the diocese;

    Do they give catechetical instructions if the ordinary has requested it in accordance with canon 1334;

    What habit do they wear when travelling about?

79. If there are any religious who collect alms, whether men or women, do they observe the prescriptions of canons 621, 622, 624; has anything untoward occurred or is there anything concerning this matter that calls for further comment?

80. If there exists in the diocese some congregation of diocesan approval, or a society of men or women living in common without vows, the ordinary shall list the name of the group or groups, its purpose, the number of its members, its usefulness, and any other pertinent facts that should be known.

81. The ordinary shall report whether he has experienced anything disagreeable with the religious in the exercise of his jurisdiction.

82. If there are any religious in sacred orders who have been granted an indult of exclaustration or of secularization, or who have been dismissed from their institute, the ordinary shall report what must be said concerning them in accordance with canons 639, 640, 669, ff.

83. Concerning women religious in particular, the ordinary shall report:
   a) are the canonical laws observed regarding admission to the novitiate, profession, the cloister, confessors and the administration of temporal goods according to canons 512, 513, 520-527, 533-535, 547, 550, 552, 600-605;
   b) If there are any monasteries of nuns under the jurisdiction of regular superiors, are they in the cases that are indicated in the law subject to the ordinary according to canons 500, § 2, and 615;
   c) To what different works do these religious groups who follow the active life devote themselves, and with what measure of success;
   d) If there are any who assist the sick in private homes or do domestic work in hospitals, Seminaries or similar houses of men, is due precaution taken for the avoidance of dangers which are recognized under these circumstances, and has anything of a deplorable character occurred?

Section 11. The Faithful

84. In a general way, indicate the character of the people's morals; of their private Christian family life; of their public Christian life in the towns and cities; whether it is based more on external pomp and solemnities than on a true spirit of piety. If there are notable differences between one place and another, indicate them.

    What is being done to encourage a return to the practice of a Christian way of life, if it has been abandoned to some extent or has digressed from the correct way?

85. What respect do the people manifest towards clerics, and especially to the bishop and the Supreme Pontiff (Canon 119)?

86. How do the people observe:

canon 1248 regarding the precept of hearing Mass and of abstaining from servile works on Sundays and on other feast days of obligation;

canons 1252, 1254 concerning abstinence and fast;

canon 770 regarding the solicitude the faithful should have for the baptism of infants;

canon 859 with respect to paschal Communion; how many men and women, in proportion to every one hundred of the faithful, are there who profess themselves Catholics and nevertheless neglect that duty;

canon 863 in reference to frequent Communion;

canons 865 and 944 concerning the last sacraments; are there among those who are considered Catholics any who defer receiving these sacraments, neglect them or even refuse them? Indicate their number in proportion to every hundred of the faithful;

canons 1203, 1239, ff. with reference to the condemnation of cremation and regarding the holding of funerals? Indicate, observing the same proportions as above, how many of those who are called Catholics are buried with merely civil or non-religious funerals. Does that happen because too large a funeral stipend is demanded or does it arise from some other cause?

87. In reference to matrimony: are purely civil marriages, concubinous unions and divorces in vogue, and in what proportion; have evil influences against the sanctity of marriage crept in; what measures have been taken in correction and for the obviation of these conditions?

88. Where Catholics live among non-Catholics, and where mixed marriages obtain, list the absolute number of these marriages and then their number in relation to non-mixed (Catholic) marriages. What harm has come to religion as the result of these unions;
Are the prescriptions of canon 1061 observed by the ones who contract such marriages?

89. Concerning the Christian education of the children:

In general, how do parents and those who take the place of parents, satisfy at home the most serious obligation to which canons 1113 and 1372 refer; What care is taken that the faithful do not become remiss in this duty?

90. Concerning schools:

In public schools, especially in the elementary grades, is the law of canon 1373 observed in regard to the religious instruction of the children; If this is not done, what is the cause?

Is due care being taken by the faithful and the clergy in the establishing of parochial schools for Catholic children and in directing them away from non-Catholic, secular or mixed schools according to canon 1374?

91. Concerning the condition and state of the parochial schools, especially the elementary grades, indicate precisely how they are supported; how many students attend them, and with what success.

And if parochial schools cannot be established, give the reason.

Indicate also whether through various "after school" endeavors, that is, by way of study clubs, of Marian congregations, of catechetical schools and by other ways, every possible means is taken in the task of safeguarding the innocence of young boys and girls.

92. Concerning religious and pious associations of the laity:

Are there any third orders secular in the diocese, and confraternities, especially those of the Most Blessed Sacrament and of Christian Doctrine, and other pious unions, in particular such as are established for the young;

What is their number, and what advantage has come to religion as a result of their work?

93. Do these associations observe the prescripts of:

canon 690 concerning subjection to the local ordinary;

canon 691 concerning the manner of their administration.

94. Are there current among the Catholic people, what are designated as "social" associations, made up of farmers, of working men, or of women who have banded together for some charitable purpose or for mutual assistance; are there asylums for infants, homes for children and for immigrants under the patronage of the Church, clubs for the young, workshops for the artisan, or for girls, etc.; in what spirit are they conducted; do they reflect docility in their subjection to the direction and guidance of the ordinary and of the Apostolic See; what benefits, moral or temporal, do they offer?

95. Is care being taken that they who belong to these associations, religious, pious or social alike, are properly instructed in Christian doctrine and lead good Christian lives.

96. Are obscene, irreligious, modernistic or liberal newspapers or periodicals current in the diocese, and how extensive is their influence; are books of this kind also widespread;

    What has been done in restraint of such an evil, and what success has marked these efforts?

97. Are there in the diocese any persons affiliated with the sect of the Masons, or any Masonic lodges; how great and of what kind is their activity to undermine religion; what is being done for the counteracting of this evil?

98. Are there any socialistic groups in the diocese; what is their number, of what importance are they, what harm have they caused religion, and what has been done for the correction of this?

99. In the exercise of their political and civil rights, do the Catholic faithful look out for the good of religion and the freedom of the Church to the best of their ability?

Section 12. A Synoptical Judgment of the Ordinary Regarding the State of His Diocese

100. Finally, the ordinary shall indicate in a summary manner, especially in his first report, what his opinion is regarding the material and moral condition of the diocese, what hope there is for improvment, and what major hazards impend.

In the subsequent reports, the ordinary shall indicate in what manner and with what success he has followed the directions and mandates of the Sacred Congregation if any have been proposed in response to his previous report. He shall further testify whether there is manifest any progress, any retrogression or rather almost the same continuing status with reference to matters of faith and morals in the diocese. Lastly, he shall suggest what causes are thought to be the basis of these respective situations.

CHAPTER VI

NON-OBSERVANCE OF THE LAW

ARTICLE I. IMPEDIMENTS EXCUSING FROM THE LAW

The Code of Canon Law makes no mention of any causes which might excuse an ordinary from the performance of this duty. That it is a serious obligation is demonstrated by the constant teaching of the Church. The very purpose which it serves, by enabling the Holy Father to perform more efficiently the commission which Christ gave the first Pope, "Feed My Lambs; Feed My Sheep," emphasizes its importance. In the Constitution *Romanus Pontifex,* which is the basis of the present law, Sixtus V used the following words to impose this duty on ordinaries: *"Iubemus igitur in virtute sanctae obedientiae."*[1] Benedict XIV confirmed that command a century and a half later by using the identical words[2] Moreover, in the old law the severe penalties threatened for its non-observance,[3] the unanimous teaching of the authors, the fact that prelates obligated themselves by means of an oath to the performance of this task[4]—all these are indications of the gravity of the obligation. Any reason, therefore, which an ordinary would consider sufficient to excuse him from the performance of this serious duty would of necessity have to be equally grave.

In the strict sense, however, there can be no true impediments which would excuse a bishop *in perpetuum* from sub-

[1] Sixtus V, const. *Romanus Pontifex,* 20 dec. 1585, § 7—*Fontes,* n. 156.

[2] Benedictus XIV, const. *Quod Sancta,* 23 nov 1740, § 10—*Fontes,* n. 303.

[3] *Loc. cit.;* Sixtus V, const. *Romanus Pontifex,* 20 dec. 1585,§ 8—*Fontes,* n. 156.

[4] *Supra,* p. 45.

mitting a report. If such were the case, a bishop would no longer be able to act in the capacity of an ordinary, and the Holy See would take steps to appoint a coadjutor to assist him. The coadjutor could assume the duties of the ordinary and consequently a report could then be prepared.[5]

There could be impediments *ad tempus,* e.g., serious illness, accident, war, etc., which the Holy See recognizes. When such circumstances arise and it is impossible to fulfill this duty, it is the accepted practice for the ordinary to inform the Apostolic Delegate of the impediments. He in turn notifies the Sacred Consistorial Congregation.

In the old law, there were those bishops who believed that they were dispensed from presenting a subsequent report when the Sacred Congregation failed to answer their previous one. Bouix[6] pointed out, however, that the law commanded the performance of the duty at certain specified times and that there was no condition attached, e.g., "provided that the Holy See replies before the next report is due." The scope of the law was not, as some bishops erroneously alleged, that appropriate replies would be dispatched in answer to their questions or demands. Rather, the purpose of the *relatio* was to inform the Supreme Pontiff on the condition of the dioceses throughout the world. Such allegations are as futile and incorrect today as they were under the old law.

Likewise under the old law a definite procedure was outlined which a bishop was to follow in the event he was lawfully impeded from fulfilling the *ad limina* visit and presenting the report. In those earlier years, the duty of submitting a report was always performed concomitantly with that of visiting first the tombs of the Apostles and then the reigning Pontiff as a demonstration of respect and loyalty. These obligations, although encompassing distinct acts, were considered species of a generic whole. As a result, those circumstances which were judged as legitimate-

[5] Cf canon 351, § 2, for the duties of the coadjutor.

[6] *Tractatus de Episcopo,* I, 64.

ly preventing a bishop from travelling to the Eternal City were accepted also as reasons excusing hm from presentin a report.

The present legislation of the Code, however, has established the duty of the quinquennial report as an obligation distinct from that of the *ad limina* visit. This is evidenced by the law of the Code which, while indeed it commands a Roman visitation every five years,[7] grants to those ordinaries who live outside of Europe the option of performing the *ad limina* visit every ten years, or in alternate quinquennial periods. The *relatio,* however, must always and everywhere be submitted every five years.[8] When these optional periods occur, the bishop is permitted to remain in his diocese, but the report must be forwarded to the Holy See.

Furthermore, even in Europe where the visit must always be made in the same year as the presentation of the report, a set of circumstances could be envisaged whereby an ordinary would be excused from the visitation and yet the Holy See would demand a *relatio.* Hostilities or natural disturbances in the territory of the ordinary or in Italy would be examples. Here would be instances when impediments which might excuse an ordinary from making a journey to Rome would not relieve him of the duty of submitting a quinquennial report.

Finally, canon 342 directs what a bishop is to do in the event he is justifiably impeded from performing the *ad limina* visit. There is in canon 340 no similar provision which has reference to the report.

Since it seems, therefore, to have been the intent of the legislator to establish the duty of the report as an obligation separate and distinct from that of the *ad limina* visit, those reasons which may excuse from the performance of the latter law are not equally applicable to the former.

As an aid in determining the lawfulness of the reason that excuses from this law, it must be remembered that,

[7] Canon 341, § 1.

[8] Canon 340, § 1.

before any cause can excuse from making the report, it must itself be of a gravity that reflects a due proportion to the gravity of the law itself.

Article II. Penalties

Pre-Code legislation directed that, if bishops failed to observe the duty of the *ad limina* visit AND the report either personally or through a procurator within the specified time, they were subject to the following automatically incurred penalties: suspension from entering their churches; suspension from administering the temporal and spiritual affairs of the diocese; suspension from any revenues deriving from the churches.[9]

The Code, however, does not establish any penalties for the deliberate non-observance of the particular duty of the quinquennial report. In the former law, it must be remembered that the *ad limina* visit and the report were considered as constituting one duty. The Code, however, makes a clear distinction between these two obligations. It is now the practice of the Roman Curia, after giving due consideration to the individual circumstances, to decide each case separately. Needless to say, repeated and obstinate refusal to abide by the directions of the Holy See in this matter could bring severe penalties upon an ordinary—even removal from office.

There need be no doubt, however, with reference to any continued binding force on the part of the penalties contained in the old law as regards this duty. It has been specifically determined that the "penalties no longer mentioned in the Code, whether spiritual or temporal, corrective (*medicinales*) or the so-called punitive penalties (*vindicative*), whether incurred *ipso facto* (*latae sententiae*), or after a judicial sentence (*ferendae sententiae*), shall be regarded as abrogated."[10]

The legislator perhaps saw fit not to establish any penalties in regard to this law in view of the distinguished

[9] *Supra*, pp. 56, 57, 60.

[10] Canon 6, 5°.

persons bound by the duty and in consideration of the very nature of the law itself. As to the content of the report, honesty, clarity and completeness seem assured through the dignity of these successors of the Apostles.[11]

If any suppression of the truth (*subreption*) or injection of a falsehood (*obreption*) should creep into the preparation of the report, the guilt of the ordinary will be determined more by the laws of Moral Theology and his own conscience than by any norm of the Code.

[11] Cf. Petition for Privilege of Portable Altar, Bouscareu, *Digest*, III, 329.

CONCLUSIONS

1. No particular year nor any act of legislation can be set down as marking the starting point of the obligation of submitting the quinquennial report. Its growth was gradual, and the legislation as it exists today did not take definite form or become a universal law until the end of the eleventh century.

2. Pope Sixtus V (1585-1590) established the obligation in a manner that could ensure its performance with becoming uniformity and regularity. This legislation is the basis of the law now contained in the Code.

3. Only episcopal ordinaries or residential bishops who possess actual jurisdiction over a defined territory are subject to the law of the quinquennial report.

4. A *coadiutor datus personae inhabili,* a permanent apostolic administrator, an abbot *nullius* and prelate *nullius,* and also a vicar apostolic and a prefect apostolic are considered by the Code as ordinaries, and hence are bound to the prescriptions of canon 340.

5. A *coadiutor datus personae habili,* a *coadiutor datus sedi,* a diocesan administrator (vicar capitular), and also the temporary apostolic administrator are exempt from the obligation of presenting a report every *quinquennium.*

6. The Law does not command nor does the *praxis* of the Holy See indicate any particular time during the 'quinquennial year' for the presentation of the report.

7. The time for the fulfillment of the obligation expires with the completion of the last day of the designated year.

8. The Code does not demand that a bishop make a report for his predecessor—whatever the cause of its omission.

9. According to the norm of the law, the report is to be "*quinquennalis*" and not "*septennalis,*" etc. If a bishop, therefore, avails himself of the exception contained in canon 340, § 3, he would be obligated to report only for a five-year period when preparing the *relatio* for the next term.

10. There are no true impediments which serve to excuse a bishop *in perpetuum* from submitting a report. There could be impediments *ad tempus* which the Holy See recognizes.

11. The Code does not establish automatically incurred penalties for the neglect of this duty. The *praxis Curiae* is to decide each case separately.

12. The measure of culpability attaching in any case of subreption or obreption in the preparation of the report is not determined by any canon of the Code; it looks to the principles of moral theology and the conscience of the ordinary for a proper appraisal.

BIBLIOGRAPHY

Sources

Acta Apostolicae Sedis, Commentarium Officiale, Romae, 1909-1929; Civitate Vaticana, 1929-

Acta et Decreta Concilii Plenarii Americae Latinae in Urbe Celebrati, A.D. MDCCCXCIX, Romae, 1902.

Acta et Decreta Concilii Plenarii Baltimorensis III, A.D. MDCCCLXXXIV, Baltimorae: John Murphy, 1886.

Acta et Decreta Sacrorum Conciliorum Recentiorum, Collectio Lacensis, 7 vols., Friburgi Brisgoviae, 1870-1892.

Augustinus, Antonius, *Antiquae Decretalium Collectiones Commentariis et Emendationibus Illustratae*, Parisiis, 1621.

Bouscaren, T. Lincoln, *The Canon Law Digest*, 3 vols., Milwaukee, Wis.: The Bruce Publishing Co., 1934-1943-1954.

Bruns, Hermann, *Canones Apostolorum et Conciliorum Saeculorum IV-VII*, 2 vols., Berolini, 1839.

Bullarum Diplomatum et Privilegiorum Romanorum Pontificum Taurinensis Editio, 24 vols. et Appendix, Augustae Taurinorum, 1857-1872.

Codex Iuris Canonici Pii X Pontificis Maximi iussu digestus, Benedicti Papae XV auctoritate promulgatus, Praefatione, Fontium Annotatione et Indice Analytico-Alphabetico ab Emo Petro Card. Gasparri Auctus, Romae, Typis Polyglottis Vaticanis, 1917; reimpressio, 1934.

Codicis Iuris Canonici Fontes, cura Emi Petri Card. Gasparri editi, 9 vols., Romae (postea Civitate Vaticana): Typis Polyglottis Vaticanis, 1923-1939. (Vols. VII-IX, ed cura et studio Emi Iustiniani Card. Serédi).

Collectanea S. Congregationis de Propaganda Fide, 2 vols., Romae: Typographia Polyglotta S.C. de Propaganda Fide, 1907.

Collectanea Constitutionum Decretorum, Indultorum ac Instructionum Sanctae Sedis ad Usum Operariorum Apostlicorum Societatis Missionum ad Exteros, Parisiis: Typis Georges Chamerot, 1880.

Corpus Iuris Canonici, ed. Lipsiensis secunda, post Aemilii Richteri curas... instruxit Aemilius Friedberg, 2 vols., Lipsiae, 1879-1881.

Corpus Iuris Civilis, 3 vols., Berolini, 1928-1929. *Codex Iustinianus*, quem recognovit et retractavit P. Krueger, ed. sterotypa 10., 1929.

Decretales D. Gregorii Papae IX, suae integritati una cum glossis restitutae, cum privilegio Gregorii XIII, Pont. Max., et Aliorum Principum, Romae, 1582.

Decretum Gratiani emendatum et notationibus illustratum cum glossis, Gregorii XIII, Pont. Max., iussu editum, 2 vols., Romae, 1592.

Denzinger, Heinrich, Bannwart, Clemens, et Umberg, Joannes, *Enchiridion Symbolorum, Definitionum et Declarationum, de Rebus Fidei et Morum,* 10. ed., Friburgi Brisgoviae: Herder, 1908.

Duchesne, Louis, *Le Liber Pontificalis,* 2 vols., Paris, 1884-1892.

Hardouin, Jean, *Acta Conciliorum et Epistolae Decretales ac Constitutiones Summorum Pontificum,* 12 vols., Parisiis, 1714-1715.

The Holy Bible, Douay Version, New York: Douay Bible House, 1942.

Jaffé, Philippus, *Regesta Pontificum Romanorum ab condita Ecclesia ad annum post Christum natum MCXCVIII,* ed. 2., correctam et auctam auspiciis Gulielmi Wattenbach, curaverunt F. Kaltenbrunner, P. Ewald, S. Loewenfeld, 2 vols., Lipsiae, 1885-1888.

Labbaeus, P., Cossartius, G., *Sacrosancta Concilia ad regiam editionem exacta,* 17 vols. in 18, Parisiis, 1671-1672.

Liber Sextus Decretalium D. Bonifacii Papae VIII, suae integritati cum Clementinis et Extravagantibus, earumque Glossis restitutis, Romae, 1582.

Mansi, Joannes, *Sacrorum Conciliorum Nova et Amplissima Collectio,* 53 vols. in 60, Parisiis, 1901-1927.

Monumenta Germaniae Historica, Legum Sectio III, *Concilia,* Tomus II, *Concilia Aevi Karolini,* recensuit A. Werminghoff, Hannoverae et Lipsiae: Impensis Bibliopolii Hahniani, 1896.

——— *Gregorii VII Registrum, Epistolae Selectae,* Tomus II, 2 fasc., ed. Erich Caspar, Berolini: apud Weidmannos, 1920-1923.

——— *Epistolae Selectae, Tomus I, Bonifatii et Lulii Epistolae, ed.* Michael Tangl, Berolini: apud Weidmannos, 1916.

——— *Epistolarum Tomus VI, Epistolae Karolini Aevi IV,* ed. Ernestus Perels, Berolini: apud Weidmannos, 1925.

Pallottini, Salvator, *Collectio Omnium Conclusionum et Resolutionum Congregationis Concilii ab anno 1564 ad annum 1860,* 17 vols., Romae, 1868-1893.

Pontificale Romanum Summorum Pontificum iussu editum a Benedicto XIV et Leone XIII Pont. Max., recognitum et castigatum, 2. ed., New York: F. Pustet, 1908.

Thaner, F., *Anselmi Lucensis Collectio Canonum una cum Collectione Iussu Instituti Savignani,* 2 vols., Oeniponte, 1906-1915.

Reference Works

Abbo, J. A.,—Hannan, J. D., *The Sacred Canons,* 2 vols., St. Louis: B. Herder Book Co., 1952.

Andreucci, Andreas H., *Hierarchia Ecclesiastica in Varias Suas Partes Distributa et canonico-theologice Exposita*, 2 vols., Romae: G. Salomoni, 1766.

Andrews, E. A., *A Copious and Critical Latin-English Lexicon*, New York: Harper & Bros., 1870.

Augustine, Charles, *A Commentary on the New Code of Canon Law*, 8 vols., Vol. II, 3. ed., St. Louis: B. Herder, 1919.

——— *Rights and Duties of Ordinaries*, St. Louis: B. Herder, 1924.

Ayrinhac, H. A., *Constitution of the Church in the New Code of Canon Law*, New York: Longmans, Green & Co., 1929.

Benedictus XIV (Prospero Lambertini), *De Synodo Dioecesana*, 2. ed., 2 vols., Parmae, 1764.

Benko, M. A., *The Abbot Nullius*, The Catholic University of America Canon Law Studies, n. 173, Washington, D.C.: The Catholic University of America Press, 1943.

Berardi, C. S., *Gratiani Canones*, 3 vols. in 4, Venetiis: Ex Typographia Petri Valvensis, 1778.

Beste, Uldaricus, *Introductio in Codicem*, 2. ed., Collegeville, Minn.: St. John's Abbey Press, 1944.

Bouix, D., *Tractatus de Episcopo*, 2 vols., Parisiis, 1859.

Cappello, Felix, *De Visitatione Sacrorum Liminum et Dioeceseon*, 2 vols., Romae: Pustet, 1912.

——— *Summa Iuris Canonici*, 3 vols., Romae: apud Aedes Universitatis Gregorianae, Vols. I & II, 4. ed., 1945; Vol. III, 1940.

Catalanus, Josephus, *Pontificale Romanum*, 3 vols., Parisiis, 1850.

Chelodi, I., *Ius Canonicum de Personis*, 3. ed., curavit Pius Ciprotti, Trento: Libreria Moderna Editrice, 1942.

Cicognani, Amleto, *Canon Law*, 2. ed., Reprint, Westminster, Maryland: The Newman Press, 1949.

Cocchi, Guidus, *Commentarium in Codicem Iuris Canonici*, 8 vols. in 5, Vol. III, 4. ed., Taurinorum Augustae: Marietti, 1940.

Coronata, Matthaeus Conte a, *Institutiones Iuris Canonici*, 5 vols., Vol. I, 2. ed., Taurini-Romae: Marietti, 1939.

Dictionnaire de Droit Canonique, Paris: Letouzey et Ané, 1924-

Du Cange, Carolus du Fresne, *Glossarium ad Scriptores Mediae et Infimae Latinitatis*, 6 vols., Parisiis, 1933.

Fagnanus, Prosper, *Ius Canonicum seu Commentaria Absolutissima in Quinque Libros Decretalium*, 5 vols. in 3, Venetiis: apud Paulum Balleonium, 1709.

Ferreres, Joannes B., *Institutiones Canonicae*, 2. ed., 2 vols., Barcinone, 1920.

Ferraris, Lucius, *Prompta Bibliotheca Canonica, Iuridica, Moralis, Theologica, necnon Ascetica, Polemica, Rubristica, Historica*, ed. novissima, 9 vols., Romae, 1885-1899.

Forcellini, A., Facciolati, J., et Furlanetti, J., *Lexicon Totius Latinitatis*, 5 vols., Patavii, 1871,

Gonzalez-Tellez, Emmanuel, *Commentaria Perpetua in Singulos Textus Quinque Librorum Decretalium Gregorii IX*, 5 vols., Lugduni, 1673.

Hallier, F., *De sacris electionibus et ordinationibus ex antiquo et novo Ecclesiae usu*, 3 vols., Romae: Mainardi, 1740.

Hostiensis, Cardinalis (Henricus de Segusio), *Commentaria in Quinque Decretalium Libros*, 5 vols., Venetiis, 1581.

Hughes, Philip, *A History of the Church*, 3 vols., New York: Sheed & Ward, 1934, 1935, 1947.

Innocentius IV, *In Quinque Libros Decretalium Commentaria*, Venetiis, 1570.

Ioannes Andreae, *In Quinque Decretalium Libros Novella Commentari*, 5 vols., Venetiis, 1581.

Jaeger, L. A., *The Administration of Vacant and Quasi-Vacant Episcopal Sees in the United States*, The Catholic University of America Canon Law Studies, n. 55, Washington, D.C.: The Catholic University of America, 1929.

Lucidi, Angelus, *De Visitatione Sacrorum Liminum*, 3. ed., a Josepho Schneider, 3 vols., Romae, 1883.

Lynch, G. E., *Coadjutors and Auxiliaries of Bishops*, The Catholic University of America Canon Law Studies, n. 238, Washington, D.C.: The Catholic University of America Press, 1947.

Martin, Conrad, *Omnium Concilii Vaticani Documentorum Collectio*, 2. ed., Paderbornae, 1873.

Melchers, Paulus Cardinalis, *De Canonica Dioecesium Visitatione cum Appendice de Visitatione Sacrorum Liminum*, Coloniae ad Rhenum, 1893.

Migne, Jacques Paul, *Patrologiae Cursus Completus, Series Graeca*, 161 vols., Parisiis, 1857-1866.

——— *Patrologiae Cursus Completus, Series Latina, 221 vols.*, Parisiis, 1844- 1864.

McDonough, T. J., *Apostolic Administrators*, The Catholic University of American Canon Law Studies, n. 139, Washington, D.C.: The Catholic University of America Press, 1941.

McElroy, F. J., *The Privileges of Bishops*, The Catholic University of America Canon Law Studies, n. 282, Washington, D.C.: The Catholic University of America Press, 1951.

Ojetti, B., *Synopsis Rerum Moralium et Iuris Pontificii*, 3. ed., 3 vols. and Index, Romae, 1909-1914.

Panormitanus, Abbas (Nicholas de Tudeschis), *Commentaria in Quinque Libros Decretalium*, 5 vols. in 7, Venetiis, 1588.

Paucapalea, Summa des Paucapalea über das Decretum Gratiani, ed. J. F. von Schulte, Giessen: Roth, 1890.

Pastor, Ludwig, *History of the Popes*, 40 vols., (1891-1953), Vol. XXI, ed. by R. F. Kerr, St. Louis: B. Herder Book Co., 1932.

Raus, J. B., *Institutiones Canonicae iuxta Novum Codicem Iuris pro Scholis vel ad Usum Privatum synthetice Redactae*, 2. ed, Parisiis: Emmanuelis Vitte, 1931.

Regatillo, E., *Institutiones Iuris Canonici*, 2 vols., Vol. I, 1946, Santander: Sal Terrae.

Romani, Silvius, *Institutiones Iuris Canonici*, 2 vols. in 3, Vol. I, Romae: Editrice "Iustitia," 1941.

Rufinus, *Die Summa Decretorum des Magister Rufinus*, edidit H. Singer, Paderborn: Ferdinand Schöningh, 1902.

Schroeder, H. J., *Disciplinary Decrees of the General Councils*, St. Louis: B. Herder Book Co., 1937.

Sipos, Stephanus, *Enchiridion Iuris Canonici*, Pécs: Ex Typographia "Haladas R. T.," 1926.

Smith, S.B., *Elements of Ecclesiastical Law*, 3 vols., Vol. I, 9. ed., New York: Benzinger, 1893.

Stephanus Tornacensis, *Die Summa des Stephanus Tornacensis über das Decretum Gratiani*, ed. J. F. von Schulte, Giessen: Roth 1891.

Thomas Aquinas, St., *Summa Theologiae*, 3 vols., Taurini-Romae: Marietti, 1948.

Thomassinus, Ludovicus, *Vetus et Nova Ecclesiae Disciplina*, 3 vols., Magontiaci, 1787.

Toso, A., *Ad Codicem Iuris Canonici Commentaria Minora*, 5 vols. in 2, Liber II, *De Personis*, Tom I, Taurini-Romae: Marietti, 1922.

Van Espen, Zegerus Bernardus, *Ius Ecclesiasticum Universum*, 5 vols., Lovanii, 1753.

Vermeersch, A.,-Creusen, J., *Epitome Iuris Canonici*, 3 vols., Vol. I, 7. ed., Mechliniae-Romae: H. Dessain, 1949.

Wernz, F., *Ius Decretalium*, 6 vols., Romae, 1898-1914; Vol. II, 1899.

Wernz, Franciscus,-Vidal, Petrus, *Ius Canonicum ad Codicis Normam Exactum*, 7 vols. in 8, Vol. II, 3. ed., *De Personis*, Romae, 1943.

Woywod, Stanislaus, *A Practical Commentary on the Code of Canon Law*, 5. ed., 2 vols., New York: Joseph Wagner, 1939.

Zitelli, Z., *Apparatus seu Compendium Iuris Ecclesiastici*, 2. ed., emendavit F. Solieri, Romae: Pustet, 1907.

Articles

Cottier, Julien, "Eléments nouveaux des normes de la visité 'ad limina' et leur valeur juridique respective, des Décrétales au Concile de Trente, *Ephemerides Iuris Canonici*, VIII (1952), 174-206.

——— "The Decree of the Sacred Congregation of the Consistory," *The Ecclesiastical Review*, XLII (1910), 326-335, 703.

——— "The *Ad Limina* Visit," *The Ecclesiastical Review*, LIX (1918), 515.

PERIODICALS

American Ecclesiastical Review, The, Vols. I—XXXII, Philadelphia, 1889-1905; *The Ecclesiastical Review,* Vols. XXXIII—CIX, Philadelphia, 1905-1943; *The American Ecclesiastical Review,* Vols. CX—, Washington, D.C. 1944-

Ephemerides Iuris Canonici, Romae: Officium Libri Catholici, 1945-

BIOGRAPHICAL NOTE

James J. Carroll was born in Columbus, Ohio, April 18, 1920. He obtained his primary education at St. Leo's Parochial School in that city. In 1934 he entered St. Charles Preparatory Seminary, Columbus, for his classical and philosophical training, and received the degree of Bachelor of Arts from that institution in 1942. He completed his ecclesiastical studies at Mt. St. Mary of the West Seminary, Norwood, Ohio, and was ordained to the Sacred Priesthood on October 27, 1945. On November 15, 1945, he was appointed assistant pastor of St. Mary's Church, Marion, and on June 15, 1947, was transferred to Holy Family Church, Columbus, to serve in the same capacity. On June 15, 1950, he was assigned to the diocesan chancery office. He entered the School of Canon Law at the Catholic University of America in the fall of 1952. The degree of the Baccalaureate in Canon Law was awarded to him in June, 1953, and the degree of the Licentiate in Canon Law in June, 1954.

ALPHABETICAL INDEX

CANON LAW STUDIES*

358. Sesto, Rev. Gennaro J., S.D.B., A.B., S.T.L., J.C.L., Guardians of the mentally ill in ecclesiastical trials.
359. Carroll, Rev. James J., A.B., J.C.L., The bishop's quinquennial report.
360. Curtin, Rev. William Thomas, A.B., J.C.L., The plaint of nullity against the sentence.
361. Ganter,Rev. Bernard J., J.C.L., Clerical attire.
362. Goertz, Rev. Victor M., J.C.L., The judicial summons.
363. Heintschel, Rev. Donald E., A.B., J.C.L., The mediaeval concept of an ecclesiastical office.
364. Kelliher, Rev. Jeremiah Francis, S.A., A.B., S.T.L., J.C.L., Loss of privileges.
365. Mock, Rev. Timothy, C.M.M., J.C.L., Disqualification of electors in ecclesiastical elections.
366. Smyer, Rev. Francis Anthony, A.B., J.C.L., Canonical regulations regarding exposition of the Blessed Scrament according to canons 1274 and 1275.
367. Wiggins, Rev. Urban C., A.B., J.C.L., Property laws of the State of Ohio affecting the Church.

* For a complete list of the available numbers of this series apply to the Catholic University of America Press, 620 Michigan Ave., N.E., Washington (17), D.C., for a general catalogue.

www.ingramcontent.com/pod-product-compliance
Lightning Source LLC
LaVergne TN
LVHW050222080826
844660LV00012B/455

* 9 7 8 0 8 1 3 2 2 5 2 6 5 *